FALSE DOCTRINES   POLITICAL POWER

THE
ANTICHRIST
DECEPTION

Do political forces use doctrine
to control Christians?

MONICA BENNETT-RYAN

IN HIS NAME
PUBLISHING
PUBLISHED IN AUSTRALIA

THE
ANTICHRIST
DECEPTION

ISBN: 978-0-6457906-4-1

© 2023 Monica Bennett-Ryan

IN HIS NAME
PUBLISHING

IN HIS NAME PUBLISHING
www.inhisname.com.au

Cover Design

MONICA BENNETT-RYAN

Photography

BRONWEN RUSSELL
www.bronsdesign.com.au

Free for download through Kindle Unlimited. Also available in Ebook, Paperback and Hardcover. Direct any enquiries to: editor@inhisname.com.au

A light shines
in the darkness,
and the
darkness has not
overcome it.

- John 1:1-3 -

CONTENTS

WHY CAN'T WE SEE THE ANTICHRIST?

INTRODUCTION

Are we seeing
what we should see?
Or is it an illusion?

CLASSIC MISDIRECTION

Do political forces manipulate doctrine and use it to control Christians? I believe so! Is manipulated doctrine currently being used to control the vast and highly influential Christian population? I believe so!

This book exposes and shatters with Scripture the false doctrine currently being used to deceive the elect and shines a bright and powerful spotlight on the political motives behind the deception.

Can the elect be deceived into falling for a false doctrine? Yes, we can! It is possible! But who would do such a thing? It's not beyond the realms of our intelligence to consider that a band of unscrupulous people, for political gain, might decide to cash in on Revelation's well-known concepts and use them to their advantage. What if I told you they already have?

Many Christians today are waiting for a demonic Antichrist to appear and rule the world through his one-world government. But what if there is no such person? What if we have been deliberately fooled into looking in the wrong direction? What if the antichrist is not a single human political leader but a way of thinking?

In recent decades, a proud and unholy false doctrine has permeated the church, subtly creating an 'image' in many people's minds that Satan is more powerful than Christ.

A beastly image!

It has made many people wonder, *"Who is like Satan? Who can wage war against him?"* It has made people all over the world think Satan's evil is too strong to fight.

That belief is the mental 'image' the beast of Revelation was set up to promote. It has no purpose but to lure people into believing Satan is too powerful to resist.

That belief is called 'worship'!

> *People worshipped the dragon because he had given his authority to the beast, and they worshipped the beast and asked, "Who is like the beast? Who can wage war against it?"* (Rev.13:4)

It is disturbing to think that Christians could have been subtly deceived into worshipping Satan, but that is the nature and purpose of deception.

What false teaching has done this? What is the classic misdirection that has fooled us into looking in the wrong direction while shrewdly leading us into Satan's trap? What false teaching could be so believable it could turn loving Christians into Satan worshippers? I'm about to tell you!

Millions of Christians have been deceived into accepting a false and polluted gospel which has them inadvertently worshipping Satan rather than Christ. It sounds horrible when put like that, but it has been successful for a time - only for a time.

That time is up!

The name of that false doctrine is the Satan-glorifying, antichrist-seeking, 'end-time' theology; you may also know it as the 'last-days' doctrine.

For all its confusing dates, times and signs, 'end-time' theology is a false gospel built around one central lie. Like a linchpin, that one lie holds all the other lies in place, and when it's removed, the whole fear-filled theology falls apart.

This book removes that linchpin, exposes the lie, and reveals those behind it!

Two spheres of influence!

There are two elements at play here: the natural and the spiritual. Satan is attempting to use one to influence the other, and Satan uses people, many people, to do his fiendish work.

In the natural world, the sole, diabolic reason behind the introduction of this false 'end-time' theology was to get Christians used to the idea of living under a Godless New World Order; to present them with a world so evil, they would believe the evil was inevitable and unstoppable.

In the spiritual world, the Satanic motive was to see Christians ditch their faith in Christ and fix their eyes on Satan instead, watching for him, thinking about him, seeking his appearance, being in awe of him and fearing his power. That's worship!

Worship of the beast!

If you have been deceived into putting your eyes on Satan instead of Christ, into being in awe of him or afraid of him, you need to read this book.

If you believe Satan and the evil in this world have become too powerful to fight, and you just want Christ to swoop in and rapture you away from Satan's evil, you need to read this book.

If you want to know what human forces are behind this great lie and how to recognise them, you need to read this book.

Without a doubt, this book will shatter the great lie at work in the body of Christ. It will destroy the power of the 'image' set up to deceive the elect into worshipping the beast of Revelation, otherwise known as 'the antichrist'. It will open your eyes to the dark forces at work in the world.

You don't have to be deceived!

This book will give you the spiritual weapons you need to combat Satan's great lie and free yourself from his insidious trap. When Christ sets you free from this lie, you will be free indeed!

> *We tear down arguments and every presumption set up against the knowledge of God, and we take captive every thought to make it obedient to Christ. (2 Cor.10:5)*

Worship of Satan
is the
beast's ultimate goal.

Everything else
is part of an
elaborate misdirection!

THIS ANCIENT KEY REVEALS THE TRUTH

CHAPTER 1

There is a key to
uncovering the truth
and it's not
hidden or new!

A SIMPLE TRUTH

The simple truth I am about to share with you will explode all the end-time confusion about that infamous Antichrist, his one-world government and his assumed post-rapture rule on the earth.

Many Christians have been taught that they can expect to be raptured just before a brutal time of terror called 'tribulation' rolls across the earth like an unstoppable tsunami. This time of terror will supposedly be more horrible than anything previously known.

We are told it will be brought to the world by a Satanic world-ruler, a single human Antichrist figure, who will rule the world from a newly rebuilt temple in Jerusalem, which, for some inexplicable reason, will be controlled by the Catholic church. Well, that's the belief...

But what if that belief is not based on truth?

What if that time of terror doesn't exist? What if there is no special time of terror? What if what we have been told about 'tribulation' does not align with Scripture? What if the need for Christians to be physically 'raptured' isn't real? What if all those end-time predictions of Satanic destruction are just part of an elaborate manipulation? What if what we have been told about the 'coming' Satanic destruction is a fantasy? How can we check?

17

The lion and lamb will be together, and a little child will lead them. (Is.11:6)

Since Biblical scholars can't agree, why don't we do as Scripture suggests and ask a little child?

Teacher: *Who does the Lamb on the throne represent?*
Child: *Jesus.*

Teacher: *How do we know it's Jesus?*
Child: *Because he died on the cross.*

Teacher: *What does God give to the Lamb?*
Child: *A scroll.*

Teacher: *Who opens the scroll?*
Child: *Jesus.*

Teacher: *What happens when he opens it?*
Child: *Horses come out, people get sick, fish die, stars fall out of the sky, there is a big earthquake, and then the world ends.*

Teacher: *Will any of this happen if Jesus keeps the scroll closed?*
Child: *No.*

Teacher: *So, who do you think is in charge of everything that happens?*
Child: *Jesus.*

Teacher: *Some say Satan makes all these things happen. Do you think that's true?*
Child: *No.*

Teacher: *Why wouldn't Satan be in charge?*
Child: *He hasn't got the scroll.*

Even a little child can see that the one who holds the Scroll of Judgment is the one who controls the judgments that come out from the scroll. This is where 'end-time' theology completely falls apart! Simple, isn't it?

This is the linchpin!

Satan and his agents are not in charge of the destruction written in the Book of Revelation! They have never been in charge and never will be!

The presumption that Satan holds the power to bring unbridled chaos to the earth is the reason for the 'rapture theory'. It's the reason for the many conflicting 'tribulation' theories. It's the reason for the supposed appearance of a single brutal 'Antichrist', and it's the reason for the 'one-world-government' scenario.

But are these concepts prophesied in Scripture as we are so often told? No! They're not! In Scripture, does Satan ever have that kind of power? No! Revelation was written to show who has absolute power.

Only Jesus holds the Scroll!

I wept and wept, for no one was found who was worthy to open the scroll or look inside. (Rev.5:4)

Then I saw a Lamb, looking as if it had been slain, standing at the centre of the throne. (Rev.5:6)

He went and took the scroll from the right hand of him who sat on the throne. (Rev.5:7)

Worthy are you to take the scroll and open its seals because you were slain, and with your blood, you purchased priests to serve our God. (Rev.5:9-10)

To believe that Satan is in charge of all the plague, famine and sword curses which come from the scroll in the hands of Christ, we must also believe that God has taken the Scroll of Judgment out of Christ's hands and has passed it along to Satan. Did that happen? No!

Will it ever happen? No!

We also have to believe that Satan, along with Christ, was found worthy by God to receive the scroll. On top of that, we have to believe that Satan, not Christ, opened it and called forth the Four Horsemen to begin the judgments. Did that happen? No!

Is it likely to happen? No!

It's dangerous to exult Satan to this position, for attributing the works of God to Satan is blasphemy!

I watched as the Lamb opened the first of the seven seals. (Rev.6:1)

It is Jesus, the Lamb of God, who was the only one in all the realms of Heaven found worthy, because of Calvary, to open God's holy Scroll of Judgment. All the judgments written in Revelation come from that holy scroll. And it is Christ who opens every seal on the scroll, one at a time.

Satan is not in charge of the judgments written in Revelation!

Satan's only role in these holy judgments of God is to be judged by Christ and thrown into the lake of fire. As for a human Antichrist, well, there is no mention of such a person anywhere in Revelation. In fact, the word 'antichrist' is not written at all in that precious book.

To believe a fictional human Antichrist, controlled by Satan, will bring the curses written in the Scroll of Judgment down hard onto the world, we have to remove all of chapter five from the Book of Revelation, for that chapter shows such a scenario is totally impossible.

Further, to believe that God will allow Satan to rule the world again after Christ died to halt his power shows total ignorance of the Gospel. Satan already had his shot at ruling the world. He lost! He will never be given another chance! God's reward to Christ for overcoming him at Calvary was kingship over all the nations of the world - forever!

Satan's rule finished at Calvary!

The kingdom of the world has become the kingdom of our Lord and of his Messiah, and he will reign forever and ever. (Rev.11:15)

Calvary is the key!

Calvary is the key to understanding all the mysteries of Revelation. Every image was given to explain to us how Christ's death and resurrection changed everything in Heaven and on Earth. And what we are shown is that all of Heaven was in awe of our Saviour's new and powerful authority.

What would Christ do next?

Before Christ went to Calvary, the final judgments for sin had already been written by God into a holy scroll and sealed with seven seals. No one in Heaven or on Earth knew the secret knowledge hidden behind those unbreakable seals. Not Satan nor any other angel, elder, patriarch, or prophet (including Daniel) knew what was written in God's sealed scroll. (1 Cor.2:7-9)

Christ had to be born a man, endure Calvary, be raised from the dead, crowned King of kings, and made ruler over the nations before he was regarded 'worthy' to open that sealed scroll. And when he began to open it, what was about to be revealed was so new and so profound there was *silence in Heaven for half an hour (Rev. 8:1)*. For the first time in Heaven's history, all praise for God ceased as everyone held their breath. The anticipation was overwhelming!

The Scroll was finally open!

The ancient mystery was
clearly revealed.

Jesus Christ would bring
a permanent end
to Satan and his agents.

YOU DON'T NEED TO BE A GENIUS

CHAPTER 2

It's not
rocket science!
No one needs
a degree
to work it out!

IT'S NOT COMPLICATED

Revelation is not a complicated book. It was written to ordinary people living around 2000 years ago. Those people didn't have the education we have today; those were much simpler times.

So why do so many educated people of today believe that only scholars can interpret the message of the Book of Revelation?

Is it because the 'scholars' themselves have deliberately made people dependent on them by complicating what is written? Have they been plying us with so many contradictory 'additions' and theories that the simple beauty of what is actually written in the Book of Revelation can no longer be seen?

I believe so!

The Apostle John wrote the Book of Revelation expecting that everyone who read it would be able to understand the meaning: educated or uneducated, young or old. Further, he expected that everyone who understood what was written would be blessed.

> *Blessed are those who hear the message of this book and take to heart what is written in it; for the time is near. (Rev.1:3)*

Is that your impression when you read Revelation? Do you feel blessed?

It's clear from the above verse that the Apostle John believed readers would be blessed by what he wrote, but are we?

These days, most people cringe when the Book of Revelation is mentioned because they don't want to hear another convoluted theory of 'end-time' doom and gloom.

John would be horrified!

Biblical 'scholars' who treat what is written in Revelation as anything but a blessing obviously have no understanding of the book's meaning. Their complicated theories and unholy 'additions' need to be tossed out.

Why do I call their multiple 'additions' unholy?

Simple! Because Christ himself is so offended by additions or changes to God's carefully worded Scroll of Judgment that he took the time to warn us, in the strongest possible terms, that he will remove his eternal blessing of Salvation from everyone who 'adds' to or 'takes from' what is written. I don't want to be one of those people, do you?

> *I warn everyone who hears the words of the prophecy of this book: if anyone adds anything to them, God will add to that person the plagues described in this book. And if anyone takes words away from this book of prophecy, God will take*

away from that person his share in the tree of life and in the holy city which are described in this book. He who testifies to these things says, 'Behold, I am coming soon!' (Rev.22:18-20)

Despite what many false teachers have said about the Book of Revelation:

- it is not about a single human Antichrist ruling the world,
- it is not about a one-world government,
- it is not about a rapture,
- it is not about the rebuilding of an earthly temple, and
- it is not about three to seven years of Satantic havoc.

Not one of the above concepts exists in the Book of Revelation! They have all been 'added'!

That is very, very scary!

What happens to those who believe and teach things that are not actually written in Revelation? Jesus has already told us plainly;

- they lose their right to enter Heaven,
- they lose their Salvation, and
- the judgments of Revelation fall on them.

Did the same false teachers who lied to you about the 'end-times' and exaggerated Satan's power also tell you that Christians can't lose their Salvation? Why am I not surprised?

Christ's personal and very direct warning at the end of Revelation is very, very scary! If it doesn't scare you, it should!

So what is Revelation about?

From start to finish, the Book of Revelation glorifies Christ. It is the testimony of his hard-won triumph over Satan at Calvary and what that triumph means. It gives us a unique glimpse into the dramatic way things changed after Christ was raised from the dead and shows us what his brilliant titles mean.

> *The revelation from Jesus Christ, which God gave him...that is, the word of God and the testimony of Jesus Christ. (Rev.1:1-2)*

> *I, Jesus, have sent my angel to give you this testimony for the churches. (Rev.22:16)*

The Book of Revelation is the personal testimony of the King of kings, given from his point of view after his battles were fought and won, and he was hailed as the victor. In his personal testimony, Christ explains why he went to war in the first place: to defend his Father's kingdom and to rescue his beloved bride.

Christ's personal testimony is filled with multiple spiritual insights that could not have been revealed to mankind before his death and resurrection. It is a treasure of Heaven, so precious that Christ had to die before it could be revealed.

Christ's strong warning at the very end of his testimony is not surprising. As the personal testimony of a mighty King, this is a royal document, a royal decree, and everyone knows a royal decree can never be altered, for death awaits those who dare.

Fascinating and beautiful!

The Book of Revelation is not complicated! It is a vibrant, fascinating, beautiful, loving and powerful book of blessings. It is packed with the brilliance and magnificence of Christ's multiple victories over Satan and his supporters and holds the greatest hope the world has ever known.

Even the detailed descriptions of the two famous beasts and the number 666 glorify Christ, as do all the other images. Christ is central to everything described in Revelation.

It is HIS testimony!

False teachers and false prophets who remove Christ from Revelation and put Satan in his place have changed the meanings of these beautiful images, making them frightening and horrible instead of instruments of praise to God for the deeply loving sacrifice of Christ. This must stop

Throw out all those horrible, fear-filled false teachings you have heard about the blessed Book of Revelation and get back to the truth. The truth is, Revelation is about the victory of our Saviour.

Revelation describes the after-effects of a loving sacrifice so profound it can only confirm our sure hope that all Christ's other promises will also be abundantly fulfilled.

His testimony vividly reveals how everything dramatically changed in Heaven and on Earth because of his death and resurrection and unveils for the first time the glorious eternal future Christ has planned for those he has redeemed.

Revelation is a love story!

From start to finish, Revelation reveals God's deep, enduring love for the world and Christ's devoted love for his Father and his cherished bride. Everything written shows Christ's enormous love for both his Father and his bride, for without that intense love, there would be no battle, no victory, and no testimony.

Every page is filled with love, but what else can we expect from the God who created love, commanded love and gave his life for love? Everything he does is based on love! He is love!

When Christ's testimony is viewed through love, all the visions, symbols and images contained within his written account lose their mystery and become clear.

Revelation is about Jesus! And Jesus is always about love!

Those
who understand
the glorious blessings
of the
Book of Revelation
can easily
explain them to
a child.

WILL THERE BE AN ESCAPE RAPTURE?

CHAPTER 3

What if the Rapture Theory is nothing more than a cruel religious scam?

TOTAL FANTASY

For those who don't know, the popular end-time Rapture Theory proposes that sometime in the near future, a special time of Great Tribulation will begin throughout the world.

This time of chaos will supposedly be overseen by a Satan-in-the-flesh, anti-Christ political leader who will rule the whole world through his One-World-Government system.

Under this Antichrist government, so the theory goes, all the prophetic destruction described in the Book of Revelation will be played out on the Earth with devastating consequences for all humanity; a kind of 'hell-on-earth'.

Meanwhile, just before the beginning of this 'hell-on-earth', Jesus will swoop down from Heaven and gather his redeemed in a glorious 'escape rapture' so they will not have to endure the terror Satan is supposedly about to unleash on the Godless inhabitants of the earth who are 'left behind'.

What a horrible story!

How can anyone think this theory glorifies Christ? Far from glorifying Christ, this teaching makes Christ look like he has no control over Satan! It totally tramples his victory over Satan at Calvary and betrays his great sacrifice!

Those who believe the lie that Christ is coming to help them escape Satan's fury have, in reality, shown they believe Satan is more powerful than Christ. They have shown they believe Satan is so terrifying he can put Christ and his bride to flight!

Christ is not afraid of Satan!

How can anyone believe, even for a minute, that a mere angel, Satan, has crushed the creator of all things, Christ, to the point where he now must take his bride and run away like a scared rabbit? Is this not horrible blasphemy? Is this not a cruel betrayal of our mighty and victorious King?

If that wasn't bad enough, there's more...

Within this blasphemous tale of betrayal, there are all kinds of mini-theories. Some believe all Christians will be raptured, and others believe some will be taken while others remain to face Satan's wrath. Then there are debates about whether tribulation will last three years or seven years and when the time of chaos might begin. Arguments abound, and confusion reigns. How ugly!

Meanwhile, there is the enormous problem of not one but two returns of Christ and two end-time resurrections. It doesn't matter a jot whether one of the resurrections is called a rapture, for (to misquote Shakespeare) a resurrection by any other name is still a resurrection.

Rapture means Resurrection!

No matter how many fanciful doctrines there may be to support a 'special' rapture before the big one on the last day, Scripture clearly teaches that Jesus will only return once.

Nevertheless, those who push this false theory tell us the first end-time return of Christ will be to gather believers only, while the final return and resurrection will be to gather everyone else for judgment. Some have even fabricated an additional theory that Christ will physically reign on earth between his two returns - though when or how he will leave again so that he can return on the last day, they don't bother to explain. Honestly! These theories boggle the mind!

Nowhere in Scripture does it say there will be two end-time resurrections or that Jesus will return twice. On this matter, Scripture is very, very clear.

Let's take a look at the facts!

1. **The last-days began with Christ**. We are not waiting for the last-days or end-times to begin, as the false Rapture Theory proclaims, but have been living in the last-days for just over 2000 years. The last-days began with Christ and were confirmed by Peter at Pentecost.

   In the past, God spoke to our fathers through the prophets. But in these last days, He has spoken to us by His Son.
   (Heb.1-2) plus *(1Pt.1:20)*

39

2. **Jesus will only return once.** This will happen at the final trump when all believers, both living and dead, will be raised at the same time. Christ stated over and over that he would raise us up on the last day of human history.

> *For my Father's will is that everyone who looks to the Son and believes in him shall have eternal life, and I will raise him up at the last day. (Jn.6:40) (Jn.6:39) (Jn.6:44)*

3. **When Jesus returns, the Earth will be destroyed.** On that day, also known as *'The Day of the Lord'*, no one will be 'left behind' simply because there will be no life on this planet after the last day. The earth will be completely destroyed on that day, and all life will cease.

> *The day of the Lord will come like a thief, the heavens will disappear with a roar, the elements will be destroyed by fire, and the earth and everything in it will be laid bare. (2 Pt.3:10)*

4. **The wicked are always 'taken'.** The days of Noah show the wicked being 'taken' to death and the few righteous 'left' alive as witnesses to the righteousness of God's sweeping judgment.

> *In the days before the flood, people were oblivious until the flood came and swept them all away. So will the coming of the Son of man be. (Matt.24:38-39)*

5. **The righteous are always 'left'.** The days of Lot show the wicked being 'taken' to death and the few righteous 'left' alive as witnesses to the righteousness of God's judgment.

> *On the day Lot left Sodom, fire and brimstone rained down from Heaven and destroyed them all. It will be just like that on the day the Son of Man is revealed. (Lk.17:29)*

6. **The 'taken' are always destroyed.** The parable of the tares and the wheat shows the tares being 'taken' first and burned and the wheat being 'left' behind after the tares are removed to be harvested last.

> *Let both grow together until the harvest. At that time, I will tell the harvesters: 'First, collect the weeds and tie them in bundles to be burned; then gather the wheat into my barn'. (Matt.13:30)*

7. **The 'left' are always saved to bear witness to God's victory.** This is confirmed again by the Apostles John and Paul, who tell us that on the last day, the wicked will be 'taken' to destruction, and only after that will those *'who are alive and left'* be caught up to join Christ in the air.

> *The angel will swing his sickle on the earth, gather its grapes and throw them into the great winepress of God's wrath. (Rev.14:17-20)*

With a loud command, with the voice of the archangel and with the trumpet call of God, the dead in Christ will rise first. After that, we who are still alive and are left will be caught up…
(1Thes.4:16-18)

8. The message of Scripture doesn't change. The same thing happened when the Israelites left Egypt. It was the wicked who were 'taken' to destruction while God's people were left to tell of his glorious salvation.

The entire army of Pharaoh followed the Israelites into the sea. Not one of them survived. But the Israelites went through the sea on dry ground. (Ex.14:28-29)

In Scripture, no wicked person has ever been or will ever be 'left behind'. The wicked are always 'taken' to destruction. The wicked always perish!

In Scripture, the righteous are always 'left' to glorify God. The righteous are always saved!

So maybe it's time to read this Scripture as it was intended to be read:

Two men will be in the field: one will be taken, and the other left. Two women will be grinding at the mill; one will be taken, and the other left. (Matt.24:41)

Knowing now what this verse really means, would you rather be 'taken' or 'left'?

42

It is simpler to
believe Scripture
than to try and follow
the ever-changing nuances
of whimsical fantasy.

TRIBULATION HAS NEVER BEEN SCARY

CHAPTER 4

There are
two tribulations,
one is 'normal' and
one is 'great'.
So, what's the
difference?

EASY TO SEE

A lot of fearful nonsense has been taught and written about a supposed time of terrible future tribulation controlled by Satan. This tribulation will, as many false teachers preach, be the reason Jesus must swoop down and rapture his redeemed. But is this true? No! Absolutely not!

Tribulation is not something that is going to magically begin sometime in the future. It has been around since Adam, and for very good reason. Tribulation is a normal part of everyday life on Earth.

What is tribulation?

The best way to know what the time of Great Tribulation will be like is to first find out what normal tribulation is and when it occurred, and the best person to teach us is Jesus.

As he was talking to his disciples about the kind of persecutions they would face during the great tribulation, he paused and made this most remarkable comment.

For this is a time of punishment in fulfilment of all that has been written. (Lk.21:22)

A time of punishment? Jesus did not call tribulation a time of 'evil', but a time of 'punishment'. The kind of punishment already written in Scripture, which people in his time already knew about and could read.

What was he talking about? What was written?

Jesus didn't leave them guessing but went on to explain how God's final judgment would work and the measuring tool that would be used on those God judged.

> *Do not think that I will accuse you before the Father. Your accuser is Moses, on whom your hopes are set. (Jn.5:45)*

Wait! Did Jesus say Moses would judge everyone? What did he mean? What does Moses have to do with great tribulation or final judgment? Isn't Moses Old Testament?

It seems that, according to Jesus, 'punishment', 'tribulation' and the 'Law of God' written by Moses are all the same. So, how does that work?

Punishment for sin!

Moses wrote the Law, and Jesus showed through his teaching and personal example that tribulation is the name given to receiving punishment for sin, specifically the punishment written in the Law of Moses and listed in the Book of Deuteronomy.

Punishment for sin, otherwise called 'the curses of the law' and generally termed 'tribulation', has happened since the Garden of Eden. It began when God judged Adam and Eve and cursed the ground because of their sin.

Moses wrote the Law of God clearly so that people could plainly see the difference between the rewards and punishments, blessings and curses, of obedience and disobedience.

God's punishment for sin has never changed.

What Christ did on the Cross was remove the punishment for sin from those who call on him for forgiveness. But that hasn't removed the punishment for sin still being poured out on everyone else.

That ongoing punishment is called tribulation!

You might be surprised to know that all those graphic judgments written in the Book of Revelation are a mirror image of the punishments of God for sin written in the Law of Moses. Please take a look at the curses in Deut.28. They are the same curses!

Most Christians these days, because of false teaching, believe tribulation has nothing to do with the judgment of God. Instead, they believe Satan is in control of tribulation. They believe it is a specific period of time rather than the trouble that comes with punishment for sin.

False prophets teach that this assumed short time period of 'evil' has somehow been delegated by God to Satan, though how and when that would have happened, they don't bother to explain.

Jesus said: All authority in Heaven and Earth has been given to me! (Matt.28:18)

To believe that Satan has control over the world, we must believe Jesus has lost control. We must believe that God has taken back the authority he gave his Son and has handed it over to Satan. Is that likely to ever happen? No! Will God betray his Son? No!

Totally false teaching!

False teachers who promote this blasphemous impression of Christ and misrepresent God's holy tribulation have a lot to answer for. Their false teaching has made Christians ineffective.

Instead of standing with Christ to 'fight the good fight', Christians now let the evil happen, believing that all the horror they see is unavoidable and merely part of the supposedly prophesied, Satan-controlled 'tribulation'. It is not!

Tribulation has never been 'evil', and evil still needs to be overcome! The truth is, we are not waiting for a specific time of tribulation to begin, for tribulation has been with us from the beginning of human history. Tribulation is normal!

Tribulation is translated in most Bibles as 'trouble'. Strong's Concordance describes the root word of tribulation as meaning to press, squeeze or afflict. In other words, 'tribulation' literally means the pressure of being squeezed by affliction, which these days we call 'stress' or 'trouble'.

Tribulation is easy to see! It's around us all the time!

Adam and Eve were the first humans to feel the personal effects of tribulation (trouble) because of their sin. This is why Jesus also said,

In the world you will have tribulation. Don't worry; I have overcome the world. (Jn.16:33)

Everyone in the world has been and will be personally affected by the consequences of sin, whether they believe in God or not.

Jesus went to the Cross to save those who believe in him from personal tribulation because of their sin! He died to save mankind from 'the curses of the Law', which is the judgment of God written in the Law of Moses, the judgment that will be carried over into the judgments of Revelation.

Until Heaven and Earth disappear, not the smallest letter, not the least stroke of a pen, will by any means disappear from the Law until everything is accomplished. (Matt.5:18)

Now, because of his death and resurrection, those covered by his blood and filled with his Spirit are protected from the direct judgment of God (tribulation/trouble) still being poured out on the world for the breaking of God's Law. Judgment that will continue via the curses of Revelation until the world ceases to exist.

This is not new doctrine! This is old doctrine! This doctrine has been believed for over 2000 years but has recently been overridden by false 'end-time' teaching. The unshakable truth is that God's Law, written by Moses, has always been the only measure of judgment for sin.

> *The Law brings down God's anger, but where there is no law, there is no breaking of the Law and no sin. (Rom.4:15)*

There are no judgments for sin attached to the New Commandments of Christ, for he *didn't come to judge the world, but to save it (Jn.3:17)*. Therefore, the only judgments for sin right up until the end of the world are those recorded in the Law of Moses.

Moses put the Law of God into writing, and Christ told us God would use no other Law to judge mankind for sin, right up to and including the final judgments at the end of time.

Satan cannot bring judgment!

The reality is that the plague, famine and sword 'tribulation' judgments of Revelation are not Satan's to play with. He has never had any authority from God to judge mankind. His only role has been to stand before God and *accuse us day and night (Rev.12:10)* so that God would have to judge us.

If he had the power to destroy us, he wouldn't be merely telling on us. He would be actively destroying us. But he's not, because he can't!

He doesn't have the power his followers would like him to have. He is the *'Father of Lies'*:

- He is not 'omnipotent'; he is only an angel; he cannot be everywhere at once - that's God's role!
- He is not 'all-powerful'; he had to conjure two beasts to do his dirty work because he couldn't manage it all himself. 'All powerful' is God's role!
- He is not 'creative'; he can't create and so can only destroy what is already created. Creation is God's role!

I could go on, but I won't. The story of Job shows that even in his heyday before Christ stripped him of his freedom, Satan still couldn't make a move against any human without God's permission.

He has even less freedom now than he had then, so the question needs to be asked, "If Satan is not in charge of Great Tribulation, then what is it about?"

What is Great Tribulation?

The time described in Revelation as the Great Tribulation is nothing more than a description of the tribulation experienced after the death and resurrection of Christ, as opposed to the tribulation experienced prior to his death and resurrection.

'Great' means more widespread, not more horrible! Despite what prophets of doom say, God's judgments/punishments/tribulations for sin will never be any worse than those listed in Scripture.

From 'Normal' to 'Great'!

Before Christ died, God could only judge people for one thing: the sin of breaking His Law. However, since the death and resurrection of Christ, God's definition of sin has broadened. God will now judge people for three things; the sin of breaking His Law, the sin of rejecting the sacrifice of His Son and the sin of blaspheming His Spirit.

> *Anyone who rejected the Law of Moses died without mercy on the testimony of two or three witnesses. How much more severely do you think a man deserves to be punished who has trampled the Son of God underfoot, profaned the blood of the covenant, and insulted the Spirit of Grace?* (Heb.10:28-29)

Though no laws are attached to Christ's New Commandment, what He brought to the world was greater than Law. He brought a New Covenant, written in his blood and sealed by his powerful Spirit.

Jesus may not judge, but his powerful Spirit does!

> *There is a judge for the one who rejects me and does not accept my words; that very word that I spoke will condemn him at the last day.* (Jn.12:47-50)

> *When the Spirit comes, he will expose the guilt of the world in regard to sin, righteousness and judgment.* (Jn16:8-11)

The Spirit of God is not just here to bless and empower us but to help us discern truth over lies. Consider for a moment what the Spirit sees when we agree with end-time mythology:

- **To agree with end-time mythology**, we have to break the Commandment to *love God with our whole heart*, which we do when we replace love for God's sovereign might and power with fear of a mere angel.

- **To agree with end-time mythology**, we have to trample the Testimony of Christ's victory over Satan under our feet, which we do when we believe Satan has the power to put Christ and his bride to flight.

- **To agree with end-time mythology**, we have to blaspheme the Spirit, which we do when we 'add' to and 'take away' from the Book of Revelation. Our alterations proudly 'correct him' and tell everyone he got it wrong. That's blasphemy! There's no coming back from that!

The Spirit of God is far more powerful than Satan can ever dream of being. His power brought the world into existence. His power cast Satan down from Heaven. His power raised Christ from the dead. His power enabled all of Christ's miracles. His is the power Satan wants but will never have.

If you believe Satan is too strong to fight and can't be overcome, you have been deceived into worshipping Satan more than God, Christ and their mighty Spirit, and you need to repent.

If you are submitting to Satan-glorifying false teachers who preach end-time blasphemy as truth, you need to flee from them and their teaching and start *worshipping God in Spirit and in truth.* (Jn.4:23-24)

The truth is that Satan's greatest weapon against the redeemed is deception, and twisting Scripture is his speciality. Inside the churches, he has an army of false teachers at his beck and call, so we need to be able to say with all God's disciples, *we are not ignorant of his devices.* (2Cor.2:11)

That's where Revelation excels!

The amazing images of Revelation warn us of Satan's plans and teach us how to overcome them:

- They warn us that Satan's first beast will be used to make war against God's Commandments and the Testimony of Christ.
- They warn us that a second beast will disguise itself as a lamb so it can easily infiltrate the churches to deliberately deceive the elect.
- They warn us about their human counterpart who emulates the two beasts and travels with them wherever they go; the Great Whore of Babylon.

Are these three evil comrades frightening? No! They have been overcome by Christ. Revelation shows us how we can join Christ in his victory and beat Satan and his minions at every turn. Revelation was given to us by God for our instruction.

It shows us how to win!

The Book of Revelation
is not about
Satan overcoming us.

It's about
us overcoming Satan!

WHO'S AFRAID OF THE BIG, BAD BEAST?

CHAPTER 5

Who is this
big, bad beast
of Revelation?
Is it the Antichrist?

HUFF AND BLUFF

The most telling and descriptive image in Revelation, which shows the absolute victory of Christ over Satan, is that famous image of the ten-horned beast.

- Is it frightening? No!
- Is it something that will cause widescale havoc on Earth? No!
- Should we fear it or its number? No!

This image was given to us by God for our instruction. The beast is described in great detail for a purpose. It comes from the sea with ten horns on seven lion heads filled with blasphemous names. It has the body of a leopard and the paws of a bear. Each of these descriptions has a meaning!

All these details explicitly show who this beast is, what it has been conjured to do and how it plans to do Satan's will. They further show that this beast is at all times under the control of God, and every believer can easily overcome the deceptions he uses against the redeemed, no matter how young, old or in between.

Satan is not the boss! God is!

Though Satan conjured it, God has placed very powerful limits on its abilities, and this beast can't work outside God's boundaries. False prophets don't want you to know this about this beast! False prophets want you to be in awe of Satan.

And I saw a beast coming out of the sea.
He had ten horns and seven heads, with
ten crowns on his horns, and on each
head a blasphemous name. The beast
I saw resembled a leopard but had feet
like those of a bear and a mouth like
that of a lion. (Rev.13:1-9)

Why are we shown this beast?

Let's start at the beginning. While reading this account in the Scriptures, it becomes abundantly clear that the description of this beast is written as a progression of previous thought, for it begins with the expression *'And I saw...'* When we trace the 'and' back to its original statement, we find the reason for the beast's existence.

The dragon went off to make war...on
those who keep the Commandments
of God and bear testimony to Jesus.
And the dragon stood on the shore
of the sea. And I saw a beast rising...
(Rev.12:17-13:1)

The first thing we notice about Satan's plans in these verses is that Satan wants to make war on the people who belong to God, but also that God has placed severe restrictions on his aggression. God has lovingly made himself and his Son the targets of Satan's rage. Though Satan may desire to destroy us, he is only allowed to attack the Commandments of God and the testimony of Christ. How loving is our God! How protected we are!

Satan cannot arbitrarily attack us at will, as false prophets would have us believe. He must remain within the boundaries set by God. This image in Revelation is the result of Satan's compliance with those boundaries. Satan is limited to tempting us to break God's Law and blaspheme the seven spiritual names of Christ. This image makes Satan's two powerful weapons abundantly clear; they are:

Sin and Blasphemy!

Immediately after we are told why and how Satan intends to unleash his rage on us, we see a beast rising out of the sea. It is no mistake that the beast has ten horns. It is no mistake that his seven heads are filled with blasphemous names.

The ten horns represent Satan's war on the Ten Commandments of God. The seven heads filled with blasphemous names represent Satan's war on the testimony of Christ, testimony that is seen in the seven names of the triumphant Spirits that crown the head of the Lamb when he appears on the throne and is made King of kings.

Satan can't win this battle. His beast's ten horns of sin are now easily overcome by the blood of the Lamb. His blasphemy of Christ's Name is now easily overcome by the word of our Testimony to Christ.

They overcame him by the Blood of the Lamb and the word of their testimony, and they loved not their lives so much as to shrink from death. (Rev.12:11)

False prophets and teachers have made millions of dollars through books, movies and podcasts that misinterpret Scripture and create fear when the purpose of this image of the beast is to destroy fear and show the awesome superiority of Christ over Satan and his plans.

This image, given to us by God, shows us that when the redeemed live in repentance and declare the glorious testimony of Christ, we overcome all the power of the beast.

Satan can't touch us!

When we understand that the image of the ten-horned beast was given to show that Satan's warfare promotes sin against God and blasphemy against Christ, we can see why the only weapons we need to overcome all his plans are the blood of the Lamb and the word of our testimony.

This means that in our battle with Satan and his beasts, our most powerful weapons are spiritual! Satan may not be able to touch *us*, but *we* have the power to destroy *his* strongholds!

> *The weapons of our warfare are not worldly. Instead, they have divine power to demolish strongholds.* (2Cor.10:4)

Instead of listening to false prophets who glorify Satan, we need to seek out true believers who can help us learn how to stand against Satan and use the mighty power of our spiritual weapons.

What else did God show us?

This not-so-terrifying beast is described as having ten horns rising up from seven 'lion' heads that are attached to a 'leopard' body with feet that look like 'bear' paws.

The lion-leopard-bear image is not a new description. The lion, leopard and bear as a threesome have a specific meaning in the Old Testament. As a group, they are only allowed to attack those who, through pride, have broken the First Commandment and forgotten God.

> *I am the Lord your God. You shall acknowledge no God but me...(but) they became proud and forgot me...so, I will come upon them like a lion, like a leopard, I will lurk by the path, like a bear robbed of her cubs, I will attack and rip them open. (Hos.13:4-8)*

By placing the horns of Satan on these animals, God is showing us that Satan is riding on the back of his will! God has permitted the beast to attack his people within definite limits; *only when they become proud and forget me.*

This is not a new understanding. It is well-known that the roaring lion has permission from God to attack those who deliberately choose to revel in sin.

This is the 'roaring lion' Jesus warned us about!

What God is describing for us in Revelation is a big, bad beast who has the loud mouth of a roaring lion, the swift body of a leopard and the razor-sharp claws of a bear. This beast is the roaring lion we were warned about, one who is roaming around, seeking someone to devour.

> *Be alert and sober-minded; your enemy, the devil, roams around like a roaring lion looking for someone to devour.* (1Pt.5:8)

The second beast is no more scary than the first beast. The role of the second beast is to twist Scripture and create false doctrines in order to bring the redeemed back under the power of the first beast.

How gracious is God to warn us. How loving is God to put such strong limits on Satan's aggression. How loving is our Saviour for going so willingly to the Cross and sending his Spirit to protect us.

God, Christ and their invincible Spirit have made overcoming Satan incredibly simple for us. Because of Calvary, we can now stand with Christ, overcome the temptations of these two beasts, and so remain free from God's judgment/punishment/tribulation.

The sure confidence we gain in looking at these amazingly detailed images, given to us by God for our protection, is the knowledge that, while ever we uphold the unassailable victory of Christ at Calvary, Satan can't touch us!

We are eternally protected!

False prophets teach
us to fear Satan.

Revelation teaches
that Satan fears
God in us!

ANTICHRIST RULER? WHERE IS HE?

CHAPTER 6

Will there be
a human Antichrist
ruling the world
through a new
one-world
government system?

THE GREAT DELUSION

So many Christians believe that a frightful human Antichrist is coming to rule the world. But is that true? There's no mention of such a person in Revelation or anywhere else in the Bible.

I honestly don't understand how biblical 'scholars' and those who say they have read the Book of Revelation can continue to push the false theory of a human Antichrist world ruler.

How can anyone possibly dismiss the most definitive statement about the identity of the ruler over all the kings of the earth stated plainly in the first chapter of Revelation? The ruler pointed out and named is Jesus Christ.

Grace and peace to you from...Jesus Christ, who is the faithful witness, the firstborn from the dead, and the ruler of the kings of the earth. (Rev.1:5)

Surely that is clear enough?

Revelation teaches over and over again that Jesus Christ is already King of kings, Lord of lords and ruler over all the kings of the earth.

Meanwhile, despite what Scripture clearly teaches, wolves in sheep's clothing insist Satan's Antichrist will (one day in the vague and distant future) suddenly appear in human form and become ruler over all the kings of the earth.

For Christians, that belief is blasphemy! Revelation makes it abundantly clear that Jesus rules the world and will continue to rule forever.

> *The kingdom of the world has become the Kingdom of our Lord and of his Messiah, and he will reign forever and ever. (Rev.11:15)*

How can those who say they love Christ ignore the clearly written message of Scripture and boldly deny his Lordship?

How can anyone say with one breath that Jesus is King over all kings and ruler over the nations, and then in the next breath, stand in opposition to Christ (anti-Christ) and agree with Satan that he, through a single Antichrist figure, will rule over all the kings of the earth in an end-time one-world government?

How can anyone believe both?

So, where did this false 'ruler' concept come from? Well, that's the million-dollar question, isn't it? Meanwhile, Satan's false prophets have been very busy! Many Christians have now been deceived into believing this lie through the deliberate mishandling and manipulation of Scripture!

> *He will set up the abomination that causes desolation. With flattery, he will corrupt those who have violated the Covenant, but the people who know their God will firmly resist him. (Dan.11:30-35)*

False teachers who push the doctrine of a human Antichrist ruling the world use the 'abomination' prophecy of Daniel to 'prove' their case.

They say the Antichrist (the abomination) will set itself up in the new temple of God, yet to be built in the current city of Jerusalem, and use its power to destroy true worship.

They say the Catholic Pope will be the savage, world-destroying, political Antichrist because the prophecy of Daniel alludes to the political power of the Roman Empire.

Despite the elaborate nature of these claims, they can't explain why a Catholic Pope would want to rule the world from a Jewish temple instead of through the already secure political autonomy and established comfort of Vatican City.

Sheer nonsense!

The whole scenario is ridiculous. Does Daniel's prophecy prove their case? Absolutely Not! If the above wasn't silly enough, the prophesied 'abomination' ruling from within a rebuilt temple in Jerusalem is old news! As a prophecy, it has already been fulfilled.

It's true that Scripture said 'an abomination' would set itself up in the temple of Jerusalem, for this was prophesied by a true prophet of God, Daniel, in the Old Testament. The problem is that prophecy was fulfilled over 2000 years ago!

The appearance of the abomination was fully manifested in Jerusalem in Jesus' day, which is why Jesus advised his disciples to flee when they saw the abomination appear.

> *So when you see standing in the holy place 'the abomination of desolation' described by the prophet Daniel (let the reader understand), then let those who are in Judea flee... (Matt.24:15-16)*

Did Christ's disciples see the abomination that causes desolation? Yes, they did! Did they flee? Yes, they did! So what did they see? They saw Daniel's prophecy coming true before their eyes. They saw the abomination at work in three distinct ways.

- The orders for the death of Christ came from the highest temple authority ruling over God's people. Those orders were an abomination.
- The temple those orders came from, where true worship was 'thrown to the ground', was a rebuilt temple in Jerusalem.
- Further, it was only because Rome governed the Holy Land that Christ could fulfil Scripture by dying on a cross, for crucifixion was a torture invented by the Romans.

Totally fulfilled!

Those three completely separate but combined circumstances (ruler in the temple, rebuilt temple, Roman Empire) completely fulfilled the prophecy of Daniel in Jesus' time.

It was clearly the abomination ruling in God's rebuilt temple in Jerusalem, under Roman authority, who threw worship to the ground by putting Christ himself to death.

There will never be any greater abomination than the killing of the creator of all things. Nevertheless, Satan's evil was turned into God's good.

If Satan had known at that time how Christ's death would backfire on him, he would never have killed the Lord of Glory.

None of the rulers of this age knew this wisdom, for if they had known it, they would not have crucified the Lord of glory. (1Cor.2:8)

How did it backfire on him?

What false prophets and false teachers will not tell you is that Satan's attempt to destroy Christ destroyed Satan instead, for after Christ conquered Satan, he was captured and held captive in chains in a place called 'the abyss'.

I saw an angel coming from Heaven with the keys to the abyss, holding in his hand a great chain. He seized the dragon, the ancient serpent, who is the devil and Satan and bound him for a thousand years. He threw him into the abyss, shut it and sealed it over him. Once the thousand years is over, he must be released for a brief time. (Rev.20:1-3)

The beast that you saw - it was, and now is no more, but is about to come up out of the abyss and go to its destruction. (Rev.17:8)

Satan is not a free agent. He is literally in jail! He can only work through his agents! When he is set free, it will only be so that he can be judged with his beasts, his whore and his followers in the outpouring of Revelation's judgments.

There is nothing in Revelation about him ruling anyone or anything again! What is waiting for him when he gets out of jail is a first-hand, up-close view of the destruction of all his ambitious plans.

This is what Revelation actually says about Satan. And this is also why he had to conjure two beasts to do his dirty work for him. He was in chains! His conjured beasts were his last desperate attempt to deceive the world!

Why did God allow this?

God hasn't finished granting Satan just enough rope to hang himself, and through the image of the ten-horned beast, we see that God himself has given Satan one last chance to destroy God's Commandments and Christ's Testimony.

Satan's God-sanctioned and limited role under the New Covenant is to create a powerful delusion, a blasphemous lie so believable it will deceive even the elect. But woe to the elect who fall for it!

The power to create this delusion is the authority Satan gave to the two beasts of Revelation, the authority and power to implement a deceptive illusion. But those who love Christ will not be fooled.

All who dwell on the earth will worship the beast - all whose names have not been written from the foundation of the world in the Book of Life belonging to the Lamb who was slain. (Rev.13:8)

These two beasts have been working together with the Great Whore to deceive all the people of the world on Satan's behalf since Satan was conquered by Christ and confined to the abyss.

The multiple deceptions of Satan, his beasts and the Great Whore are not new or confined to one generation in history but have been active in the world since before John wrote Revelation.

New generation - new tactics!

However, it is not hard to see that in the last sixty to seventy years, these three agents of Satan have unleashed the most powerful delusion ever let loose on the Body of Christ. And because of technological advances, this one deception has been able to influence everyone in the world simultaneously.

This ongoing worldwide deception loudly screams that Satan is more powerful than Christ because (supposedly) not even Christ can stop his planned tsunami of evil from happening.

Nevertheless, Christians who believe this lie and enter into its delusion will be condemned by God for not remaining faithful to Christ and not loving the truth above all else.

> *They perished because they refused to love the truth and so be saved. For this reason, God will send them a powerful delusion so they will believe the lie, and so all will be condemned who have not believed the truth but have delighted in wickedness. (2 Thes.2:10-11)*

We know we overcome Satan and his agents by the blood of the Lamb and by the word of our Testimony. But here we see what the third part of that overcoming verse means, for unless we personally love Christ with our whole heart, we will not be able to resist the lure of this great lie.

> *They have conquered him by the blood of the Lamb, by the word of their Testimony, and they did not love their lives so as to shrink away from death. (Rev.12:11)*

Sheep and Goats!

God, Christ and their all-powerful Spirit are always a thousand steps ahead of Satan. Nothing surprises them! There is no evil they can't turn to good, and that applies to every element of this vile delusion. God has granted Satan permission to have his agents spread this deception as part of the separating of the sheep from the goats.

Many people will come to the Lord at the end of the day saying, 'Didn't I do this for you?', 'Didn't I do that for you?' but God, who looks on the heart, will judge everyone by whom their works have served. That is, by whom they love.

The first and greatest Commandment is that we should love God with our whole heart, soul, mind and strength.

> *Love the Lord your God with all your heart and with all your soul and with all your mind and with all your strength.*
> *(Mk.12:30)*

Christians who love Christ will stand unshaken in their belief that Christ is the all-powerful, mighty King of kings, Lord of lords, and ruler over all the nations of the earth.

Christians who love the world will believe the blasphemous lie spread by Satan and his minions that a single human Antichrist figure will (someday) appear on earth, become the ruler of the nations, and put Christ and his bride to flight.

What do you believe?

Those who teach that Christians should look for the rebuilding of the Jewish temple in Jerusalem as a sign that the Antichrist is coming are promoting Satan's delusion. There is no rebuilt temple in Revelation, no Antichrist world ruler in Revelation, and neither Rome nor Israel are mentioned.

There will never be at any time in history a single human being so powerful that he or she will be able to banish God, Christ and their Spirit from the world they created. It is the greatest delusion to ever be given any credibility within the body of Christ.

Satan's servants, the false prophets, false teachers and other 'wolves in sheep's clothing' inside the church who help Satan spread this great lie stand condemned by the very Scriptures they pretend to uphold.

The simple truth is that Jesus Christ is and will always be King of kings, Lord of lords, and ruler over all the kings of the earth.

A quick reality check!

Meanwhile, while all this false doctrine is running rampant across the Christian world, Satan is still in jail! That's right! He can't even get himself out of the abyss! He has to be let out! Oops! No power there! Satan himself, the author of this power-mad fantasy, is the most deluded being in existence!

Despite knowing all this, false teachers continue to insist that Satan has already been let out of the abyss (as if they know when and how that happened). And so, they say, it will only be a short time before the 'man of lawlessness' predicted by the Apostle Paul will take control of the world.

I don't think so...

All false prophets
seem to be
'nice people'.

That's what makes
them so
easy to believe.

CAN ONE PERSON DESTROY THE WORLD?

CHAPTER 7

Should
'Man of Lawlessness'
or 'Man of Sin'
be interpreted as
'Ruler of the World'?

PURE CHICANERY

The whole idea of a world-destroying Antichrist is unscriptural. Lawlessness does not mean 'despotic ruler of the world'. Let's get back to Scripture.

- *Scripture has shown* that Christ, not Satan, is in charge of all the end-time plague, famine and sword judgments written in the Book of Revelation.

- *Scripture has shown* there is no human Antichrist world-ruler written about anywhere in the Book of Revelation.

- *Scripture has shown* that the prophecy of Daniel regarding a ruler in the rebuilt temple in Jerusalem under Roman authority was completely fulfilled in Jerusalem during the life and times of Christ.

- *Scripture has shown* the 'man of lawlessness' is also known as the 'man of sin'. Neither lawlessness nor sin translates to mean 'man who has the power to bring about the physical destruction of the whole world'.

So, where did the idea of a destructive human Antichrist world-ruler come from? Not from Revelation and not from the rest of Scripture. This concept is totally foreign to the Bible and is, in fact, contrary to what the Bible teaches. The concept is a perfect example of what it means to 'twist' Scripture.

The Apostle John, who wrote the Book of Revelation, is the only Apostle who ever used the word 'antichrist'. He invented the word!

John described to his disciples what 'antichrist' meant, laying down its meaning and application in writing in several Epistles. Yet when he wrote the Book of Revelation, he chose not to include that particular word on any page.

Why was that?

Why did the Apostle John leave the word 'antichrist' out of his Book of Revelation? The answer is made clear in the following Scriptures.

> Dear children, this is the last hour, and as you have heard that the antichrist is coming, even now, many antichrists have come… (1Jn.2:18)

> Who is the liar? It is the man who denies that Jesus is the Christ; such a man is the antichrist… (1Jn.2:22)

> Do not believe every spirit but test the spirits…every spirit that does not acknowledge Jesus is not from God. This is the spirit of the antichrist, which you heard is coming and even now is already in the world. (1Jn.4:1-6)

> Many deceivers, who do not acknowledge Jesus Christ as coming in the flesh, have gone out into the world. Any such person is the deceiver and the antichrist. (2Jn.1:7)

These are the only four Scriptures in the entire Bible which mention the word 'antichrist'. There are no others! They do not describe a single person but a number of people.

The Apostle John starts by saying, *you've heard the antichrist is coming*...and then goes on to say, *even now, many antichrists have come...*

So we see that even back in John's day, when the Bible was being written, the disciples regarded the antichrist as a 'spirit' who could be seen in 'many', and, most importantly, it had already made its appearance.

For us, this is all past tense!

It is absolutely clear from Scripture that the disciples of Christ had no concept in their minds of a single fearful, human, God-hating world leader who would appear at the very end of human history with the sole purpose of destroying the world.

Such a person cannot be found in Scripture!

So why do false prophets insist they have a legitimate right to keep us looking for a single human Antichrist? Simply because translators, sometime in the last seventy to a hundred years or so, changed the meaning of one single word. One word! A very timely and convenient 'error' for those with a personal agenda. This is Scripture twisting at its finest.

It's easy to check!

Was this a deliberate misinterpretation? I believe it had to be, for it flies in the face of the usual interpretation of that one word.

It is important to note here that the Greek word in the original document remains unchanged and can still be checked. It is only the interpretation written in English language Bibles that has changed.

Without this mistranslation, there would be no Scriptures at all that false prophets could use to back their blasphemous theory.

But now, because of one glaringly incorrect translation, a whole false doctrine has been ratified. It doesn't seem to matter that this manipulated translation is not backed by anything else in Scripture. It is accepted as Gospel.

2 Thessalonians 2:3

In the above Scripture, the 'man of lawlessness' or 'man of sin' has been assumed to come from the single form Greek word 'aner' (meaning a single man or a husband) and described as 'he'.

However, that is an incorrect assumption. The word actually written in the Greek is not 'aner'; it is 'anthropos', and the difference is huge.

'Anthropos' is plural. It means *belonging to mankind or humanity – multiple human beings,* and is normally described as 'they'.

Check the concordance!

The first translated interpretation of this particular Greek word *'anthropos'* was in Matt.4:1-4, where Jesus said, *'Man shall not live by bread alone...'* Jesus was not talking here about one man but all mankind. *'Anthropos'* is always plural.

This same Greek word is consistently used when Jesus speaks about himself as the *Son of man* and is commonly used to mean 'mankind' throughout the New Testament.

So why did its meaning suddenly change? Why wasn't *'anthropos'* translated the usual way in this instance? It should have been!

In the said passage, *the man of lawlessness is revealed. He...* (single) should have been translated, *the man of lawlessness is revealed. They...* (plural). In other words, rather than one man (he), humanity itself, both men and women would become lawless (they). Without this mistranslation, there would be no Scriptures at all to support a single Antichrist theory.

Translating *anthropos* correctly as 'they' instead of as a single person 'he' would have kept the meaning of the chapter in context and killed the subsequent confusion!

The whole point of this chapter was to prevent false end-time teaching from deceiving the elect. It is ironic that this particular chapter should be chosen to become the epicentre of end-time deception.

What is the context?

In this chapter, Paul explained clearly what the spirit of lawlessness in people would look like, where it would begin, its purpose, and what believers could do to protect themselves from its subtle influence.

Now, that's a lot to say in a very short passage, but the Apostle Paul considered his explanation to be enough.

He was reiterating, in a different kind of way, the same thing Christ had taught about the end being like the days of Noah and Lot.

Both those 'ends' were preceded by lawlessness and widespread rebellion, and Paul is saying Christ's return would be the same.

- **In the days of Noah,** 'everyone' was destroyed except for eight righteous who were left alive after the wicked were swept away.

- **In the days of Lot**, 'everyone' was destroyed except for three righteous who were left alive after the wicked were consumed by fire.

The point Paul was making was that 'everyone' except the faithful would be destroyed at that time.

This will happen when the Lord Jesus is revealed from Heaven in blazing fire with his powerful angels. He will punish those who do not know God and do not obey the Gospel of Jesus. (2Thess.1:7-8)

2Thes.1 (previous page) is where Paul starts his teaching about the punishment of many. So we see that 2Thes.2 is written to clarify his 2Thes.1 statement, where he indicates that everyone who is lawless will be destroyed on Christ's return.

> *Let no man deceive you by any means: for that day shall not come, except there come a falling away first, and the man of sin be revealed.* (2Thes.2:3)

Here, Paul is teaching that a widespread 'falling away' must precede the coming of Christ, for only then will Christ be able to return with great power and might to destroy with one breath all the lawless, wicked and sinful who have fallen away.

The 'falling away' and 'man of lawlessness' described in these verses are clearly not about one person, for the destruction includes all the people of the world who have rejected God and Christ!

> *Then the lawless one(s) will be revealed, whom the Lord Jesus will slay with the breath of His mouth and annihilate by the majesty of His arrival.* (2Thes.2:8)

Through both Books of Thessalonians, Paul teaches that, on his return, Christ will destroy everyone except the righteous who are left alive and ready to go with him to glory.

His message was clear until someone changed it!

The 'lawless spirit' and great 'falling away', which Paul taught must be seen on earth before Christ could return, wrongly became the rebellion of just one human being.

This deceptive interpretation has caused great confusion, for when people read the entire chapter, the first half is about a single person 'he' and the second half is about many people 'they', and Paul's teaching no longer makes sense!

However, when we remove the erroneous translation and apply the correct meaning of *anthropos,* Paul's teaching suddenly makes complete sense. It covers these questions...

What is going to happen?
Jesus will return. (v1)

When is it going to happen?
Not before the rebellion of many. (v3)

What is the rebellion going to look like?
Many people will set themselves above God's word. (v4)

Where is it going to happen?
In the church. (v4)

When will it start?
It is already at work. (v7)

Who is going to bring it?
Satan will use God's own people to promote a great lie. (v9)

Why is it going to happen?
God wants to see who is loyal to Christ. (v11)

How is it going to turn out?
The rebellious believers who stray from the truth and believe the lie will perish. (v10-12)

What can we do to protect ourselves?
Stick to the true Gospel. (v14-15)

Please note: Satan is not in control of the destruction of the wicked here - God is!

The Apostle Paul's simple solution for the Thessalonians in their battle against Satan's deception and the lawlessness it would promote, even in their day, was for them to remain loyal to the true Gospel.

Is Paul's solution ever taught?

- **Do 'end-time' prophets of doom** and gloom ever teach it is God, and not Satan, who will bring the destruction to the world? No?

- **Do the false teachers** who use this Scripture to warn of the supposed 'coming' of a single human Antichrist ever present Paul's solution to his coming? No?

- **Do the 'last-days' fear peddlers** ever explain what the 'great lie' is or teach that we can be saved from the 'antichrist spirit' and all that Satan can devise and throw at us by sticking to the true Gospel? No?

The three powerful truths revealed by Paul in Thessalonians (God destroys the wicked, lawlessness is the result of a lie, and the Gospel is the solution) are nothing like the horrific Antichrist stories running amok in Christian circles.

The beast-inspired, false 'end-time' gospel denies God is the ultimate judge of all mankind, denies Christ is ruler over all the kings of the earth, and denies the mighty Spirit of God is the power behind the true Gospel.

Instead, beastly prophets promote the false 'end-time' gospel and encourage lawlessness in God's people by getting them to exalt Satan over Christ just as Paul warned; *they will exalt themselves over everything that is called God or is worshipped...*

- **The false gospel** tells us Satan will judge and destroy all who live on the earth.

- **The false gospel** tells us Satan is the ruler over the kings of the earth.

- **The false gospel** tells us Satan is so strong even God himself cannot stop him, so Christ needs to swoop in and rapture believers away from his power.

What an unholy belief!

A proven false translation, by accident or otherwise, does not have the power to change the meaning of Scripture or support a false gospel.

Not even the altered nature of this one word in Thessalonians has the power to support the outrageous claim that Satan is more powerful than Christ! No Scripture does!

But what if...?

For argument's sake, let's assume for a moment that the translation is correct and a single 'man of lawlessness' will appear someday.

We must keep in mind that lawlessness does not mean 'absolute power' or 'world domination'. It means rebellion against the laws of God.

If a single 'man of lawlessness' did arise, he would still not resemble in any way the stories told about a destructive, Satanic, human Antichrist with the power to rule the world, banish the Spirit of God and put Christ and his Bride to flight. Such a person doesn't exist in Thessalonians or anywhere else in Scripture and never will.

Honestly? Would one person rebelling against the Laws of God and the Testimony of Christ be enough to bring about the end of the world? No!

In Thessalonians, as in the rest of the Bible, there is no human Antichrist world leader - no one-world government - no future abomination ruling from a rebuilt temple - no special time of tribulation - no Satanic controlled chaos throughout the earth, and no rapture escape from Satanic vengeance. All those concepts are made up! They are totally false!

The time of rebellion Paul was talking about in his second letter to the Thessalonians had already started in his day, according to him.

This fits with the rest of Scripture, which talks about the tribulation of the 'last days' - 'last days' meaning the time overseen by the New Covenant, by Christ's New Commandments and by the coming of the Spirit at Pentecost, all of which the disciples knew were ushered in by Christ.

Changing the meaning...

Changing the meanings of words is what false prophets do! Many words and concepts have been changed, not just the one word in Thessalonians.

- The term, 'last days' glorifies Christ's entry into the world. It does not mean 'the end of the world', but that's what false teaching leads us to believe.
- The word 'antichrist' should mean anyone opposed to the Gospel of Christ, but false teaching has everyone thinking it only applies to one person with the power to defeat Christ.
- The meaning of 'tribulation' has been changed from 'God is in control' to a future event where 'Satan is in control'.

All these changes are blasphemous. Every one of them replaces the glory of Christ with the non-existent 'glory' of Satan. That is Satan worship!

Flee this unholy teaching!

Apostle John
taught us how to
'test the spirits'
to see who is genuine
and who is not.

CAN YOU SEE THE REAL DECEIVER?

CHAPTER 8

While our eyes
search for the
Antichrist,
we miss the
real deceiver;
the Great Whore!

OUR REAL ENEMY

I find it beyond amazing that so much attention is given to a made-up figure who doesn't exist in Scripture, while the clearly defined true enemy of the Bride of Christ, who is fully described in Scripture, is completely ignored.

This kind of misdirection is a classic component of dark magic. It is Satan's way! Get the suckers focused on a created illusion while the real trickery remains hidden.

The whole Satan-fearing, end-time 'antichrist-is-coming' mythology is the flashy illusion given to take the focus off the real trickery, the only trickery that can do deadly harm to believers.

Christ warned us!

In his Book of Revelation, Christ did not mention a single human anti-Christ world ruler, yet he devoted four whole chapters to explaining the cunning, trickery and deception of his Bride's only human nemesis, revealing her relationship with the two beasts and their combined demise.

The Great Whore of Babylon!

If it was important to Christ to put such effort into warning us about the Great Whore, why are we ignoring his warning? Why are we allowing ourselves to be side-tracked by a fantasy, a mere illusion?

The Great Whore is Satan's true servant on earth and always has been! She is not a single human figure, for she has been around for centuries. She is not a church organisation or any particular nation, for she is thoroughly human and can be seen in every generation and every nation.

The great 'anti' Bride!

Satan's harlot is the opposite of the Bride of Christ in every way. In the same way that we think of Christ's bride as a single figure made up of all those who carry the Spirit of Christ, we need to think of Satan's harlot as a single figure made up of all those who carry the Spirit of Antichrist. She represents everyone who has ever rejected the Commandments of God and the Salvation of Christ.

Multitudes of antichrists!

In his warning, Jesus told us who she is, what she does, how she does it, and what we should look for. Finally, he warned us to *'come out from her'* lest we be destroyed with her when she is judged by him on the day of her very public annihilation. And his warning speaks to every generation.

> *Then I heard another voice from heaven say: "Come out of her, my people, so that you will not share in her sins or contract any of her plagues. For her sins are piled up to heaven, and God has remembered her iniquities. (Rev.18:4-5)*

Christ told us to *'come out from her!'* But what does this mean? What are we supposed to *'come out from'*? And why would we share in his judgments for her sins? What does that mean?

> *Therefore, in one day, her plagues will overtake her; death, mourning and famine. She will be consumed by fire, for mighty is the Lord God who judges her. (Rev.18:8)*

Why aren't we being warned?

Millions of Christians have been led to believe Satan's antichrist spirit will come to the earth as a single human figure for one moment in time, but that's just not true!

> *Dear children, this is the last hour, and as you have heard that the antichrist is coming, even now, many antichrists have come. (1Jn.2:18)*

While our eyes have been focused on a non-existent enemy (the future appearance of just one human antichrist), the real enemy (many human antichrists) has remained free to trap us, trick us and promote a lifestyle which could cost us everything.

The Whore of Babylon is and has always been Satan's human servant on earth. Christ expects his redeemed to recognise the Great Whore of Babylon; otherwise, he would not have told us to *'come out from her'*. Should we obey him?

Who is this Great Whore?

Basically, she is a way of thinking. We can't come out from a single 'person', but we can come out from 'herd mentality', a common way of thinking. When we understand the way our enemy thinks, we can heed Christ's warning and distance ourselves from her influence.

The whore and 'the beast' think the same way!

The ten-horned beast, the two-horned beast and the Great Whore of Babylon all work together to do Satan's will on earth. The ten-horned beast carries the woman wherever she wants to go. The three work together towards one evil goal.

> And I saw a woman sitting on a scarlet beast, covered with blasphemous names and it had seven heads and ten horns. (Rev.17:3)

This woman, a prostitute dressed in scarlet, who rides the scarlet beast, represents all the people of the world in every nation on earth.

> The waters you saw, where the prostitute was seated, are peoples and multitudes and nations and tongues. (Rev.17:15-16)

Though Satan's beasts carry the Great Whore and guide her in all her ways, they hate her with a passion. In the end, they betray her and destroy her.

The beast and the ten-horns you saw will hate the prostitute. They will bring her to ruin and leave her naked. They will eat her flesh and burn her with fire. (Rev.17:16)

In complete ignorance of their hatred, the Great Whore makes herself 'one' with the two beasts of Revelation. The three of them think the same way, act the same way and serve Satan the same way.

This is good news for us!

It means that if we understand the character of the ten-horned beast and how it thinks, we will understand the character of the Whore of Babylon, Satan's human face on Earth, and recognise her spirit in the people around us!

Can we understand the character of the ten-horned beast? We sure can! Christ spelt it out clearly. And when we recognise the living, breathing people acting according to its character, we will be able to 'come out from them'.

The first thing we are shown about the ten-horned beast is that it is not a fixed 'location' on Earth. It is walking and roaring. It has seven lion heads, a leopard body and four bear-claw feet. It is the 'roaring lion' Jesus warned us about.

Be sober-minded and alert. Your adversary, the devil, prowls around like a roaring lion, seeking someone to devour. (1Pet.5:8)

The second thing we are shown is that this beast is already defeated. Despite the fact its head was severely wounded at Calvary, it is filled with pride and sets out to gain subjects in a world Christ has ensured Satan will never rule again.

> One of the heads of the beast seemed to have a fatal wound, but the fatal wound had been healed. *(Rev.13:3)*

The third thing we are shown is that this description was given by God to glorify Christ. The beast was conjured by Satan to do one thing only. Make war against those who keep God's Commandments and bear testimony to Jesus.

> He (Satan) went off to make war on... those who keep the Commandments of God and bear testimony to Jesus... *(Rev.12:10)*

When we know the beast exists only to tear down the Commandments and the Testimony of Christ, we immediately know what we should look for in the Great Whore that it supports and carries.

What does it tell us?

The first thing it tells us is that she is roaming around, like Satan, seeking to devour our faith, hope and love for God and Christ. Like the beast, she will hunt us with speed, she will roar out lies, and she will viciously tear at our lives to get us to take our eyes off Christ.

The second thing it tells us is that she is filled with pride. No matter how many times she may be defeated, she will still arrogantly believe those who worship God and Christ are fools and will do everything in her power to prove them fools.

The third thing it tells us is that she, like Satan and his beasts, will do everything she can (using money and the buying and selling of human souls - Rev.18:13) to tempt, trick, trap or deceive us into breaking the Commandments or bringing blasphemy to the name of Jesus, or both.

'She' is people!

People who try to convince us our belief in Christ is foolish or imaginary, or try to seduce us with all manner of worldly things, or attack us with lies or persecutions, are showing the nature of the beast and the woman it carries.

We cannot appease such people. We will never convince them. We cannot agree with them. They are the ones we are called to 'come out from'!

The constant deceptions of this deadly trio are all around us all the time. Their tricks, traps and ploys are designed to get us to take our eyes off Christ, doubt his power, lose hope in him and ultimately disobey God's commands.

If we succumb to these beastly temptations, we compromise our relationships with both God and Christ and, in doing so, 'worship the beast'.

The temptations of the ten-horned beast are blunt. It promotes the outright breaking of God's commandments and the outright mockery and blasphemy of Christ.

The temptations of the great whore are wrapped in seduction. She uses human needs and the things of this world to lure us away from devotion to God and Christ.

The temptations of the second beast are the sneakiest and most subtle of all. It positions itself in God's house and breathes out lies to deceive, if possible, even the elect. Its aim? To get God's people worshipping the first beast.

The Second Beast
(same purpose, different tactics)

The second beast looked like a lamb but spoke like a dragon. It exercised all the authority of the first beast on its behalf and made everyone worship the first beast. (Rev.13:11-12)

The second beast looks like a lamb but speaks like a dragon, a wolf in sheep's clothing! It looks like a sheep, so it can easily move among sheep and deceive them with the same aim as the first beast (the roaring lion), which is to devour them.

Its job is to deceive the elect into worshipping the first beast. And God allows it to succeed for a time, to *wage war against God's holy people and to conquer them* (Rev.13:7)

How does this happen?

Precisely as the Apostle Paul describes in 2Thes.2:12, God allows the promotion of a great lie so that those who remain loyal to Christ and the true Gospel will be seen.

> They (lawless people) will oppose and exalt themselves above everything that is called God or is worshipped. (2Thes.2:4)

> They will use all sorts of displays of power through signs and wonders that serve the lie and so deceive those who are perishing. They perish because they refuse to love the truth and so be saved. (2Thes.2:10)

> Jesus will destroy the lawless with the breath of his mouth and by the splendour of his coming. (2Thes.2:8)

Satan doesn't have a physical body. He is a spirit, and his spirit is actively at work in the world through humans. This is not hard to see!

The first beast directs its attention to the world to promote sin and blasphemy among those who don't know Christ.

The second beast directs its attention to the redeemed to trick them into sin and blasphemy by default by teaching lies that promote disobedience to God's commandments and bring blasphemy to Christ.

The great whore is the army of people, both male and female, of all tribes, languages and nations who carry out the plans of the first and second beasts. They are everywhere on earth, including every gathering of Christians. Like the two beasts, their purpose is to promote sin and blasphemy.

Satan's wicked queen is the one we need to recognise. She is the one we must avoid at all costs. She is full of deceit, and her temptations are poison. She uses all the schemes of the two beasts in her attempts to destroy the Bride. She disguises herself, speaking through many different people in various ways, both inside and outside the church.

Can we see her in the world today? Yes! Clearly!

This army of antichrists mock the very existence of God, embrace sin, scoff at Christ, blaspheme the mighty sevenfold Spirit of God and use every worldly seduction available to tear down faith, hope and love and separate us from our God and King.

'She' is the human face of the beast!

The greatest deception Satan has ever achieved is fooling God's people into believing that his beasts and multitudes of human antichrists are not at work in the world now but will come to the earth sometime in the vague and distant future as just one person.

Those who fall for this evil lie and continue to look for some single 'future' antichrist figure will not be able to see the many antichrists standing right in front of them. Nor will they be able to *'come out from'* the Great Whore and the influence of her two dangerous associates.

How do we recognise her?

The Apostle John knew more about the *spirit of antichrist* than believers of his time and taught his disciples to 'test the spirits' of other Christians to see if they were genuine or antichrist. His test still applies, and it's not difficult to do.

John's test never fails, and it can't be faked. It is completely inoffensive and so gentle it is always undetectable to the one being tested. Applying it places us in the position of being *wise as a serpent but innocent as a dove (Mt.10:16)*

> *Dear friends, do not believe every spirit, but test the spirits to see whether they are from God…for many false prophets have gone out into the world. (1Jn.4:1-6)*

John understood that all false prophets and teachers in the body of Christ who secretly carried the *spirit of antichrist* and whose covert aim was to deceive the elect had one major flaw. Like their true master, the two-horned second beast, they would also *'speak like a dragon'*. And this flaw became the infallible key to John's incredibly accurate and successful test.

John's test involves the words that come from a person's mouth, words that reveal the heart of the person speaking, the fruit of their lips. It reflects Jesus' teaching that we will *know them by their fruit.*

From the fruit of his mouth, a man's heart is filled, and with the harvest of his lips, he is satisfied. The tongue has the power of life and death, and those who love it will eat its fruit. (Prov.18:20-21)

All we need to do is listen to the words coming out of other people's mouths, for their words will reveal their heart attitudes. If they love the world, they will speak from the viewpoint of the world. If they love God, they will speak about Christ, his Spirit and the beauty and wonder of his Kingdom.

If we apply this test to all teaching from pulpits, we will always recognise the false doctrine of the beast. The beast and his antichrist comrades will always give every spiritual thing a worldview. If we apply this test to every conversation, we will never fall into the wicked queen's trap of living according to the world rather than the Kingdom.

This is how we 'come out from her'!

Christ has provided his greatly loved Bride with a secret weapon so well hidden it can't even be detected by the enemy while it is being used. It is utterly invisible! How awesome is that? Only God could devise such a perfect and painless weapon!

Simply put,
if the words don't
give glory
to God and Christ,
they're not being spoken
by the Spirit of God!

THE END
JUST AHEAD

CAREFUL - SIGNS CAN BE DECEIVING

CHAPTER 9

What are
the signs that
the end is near?
Are we there yet?

A FUTILE SEARCH

So far, we've seen that Satan is not in control of the judgments of Revelation, and therefore, there is no reason for Jesus to swoop down and rapture the redeemed to safety.

We've seen that Satan's two beasts and his Great Whore work together to tear down the Commandments of God and bring blasphemy to the Testimony of Christ. And together, they make up the 'antichrist spirit' Apostle John warned us about.

We've seen that tribulation (trouble) is the normal process of Godly judgment for sin and that it has increased to 'great' tribulation since rejection of Christ and blasphemy of the Spirit have been added to the breaking of God's commandments.

However, knowing the simplicity of the true Gospel doesn't stop some people from wanting to know precisely when the end will come. They continue to hunt for signs that 'the end is near'.

All hunt - no prize!

It is because false teachers have been so effective in spreading the great lie that today, many Christians strain their eyes and minds looking for the signs that the end is near. They do this to prepare for the 'rapture', which they believe will happen before the 'Antichrist' world ruler appears and the devastating time of 'tribulation' begins.

Others, again because of false teaching, believe the signs of the times show the 'end-times' are already beginning or have begun, while others argue that we are entering the end of the end-times or the last days of the last days. Really?

That kind of religious double-talk is not from Scripture. There is no special 'end' of the end-times in Scripture. In Scripture, there are only the former days or the latter days, the past days or the last days, the Old Covenant or the New Covenant, and the Old Law or the New Law. It's either one or the other.

Blatant heresy!

The ushering in of the last days wasn't just a timeframe. It was a package deal. It came with powerful new conditions that made the former days, with all their laws and requirements, obsolete.

Claiming that there is a new 'end-times' separate from the last days ushered in by Christ means there is another package deal, another new set of laws, another new Covenant which would make what Christ did obsolete. Total blasphemy!

There are absolutely no Scriptures to support such blatant heresy! Nevertheless, that's what many false 'end-time' prophets openly teach.

- Is there a 'last of the last days' in Scripture? No!
- Is there a special 'end-times' in Scripture? No!
- Is there a warning not to think that way? Yes!

Jesus warned us!

Jesus warned us not to listen to Christian leaders or prophets who tell us 'the end is near'!

Many will come in my name saying, "I am he!" and "the end is near". Do not go after them! (Luke 21:8)

Jesus' warning is as blunt as blunt gets. The meaning is crystal clear and easy to understand. Don't believe people who tell you the end is near!

If anyone tells you they know the end is near because they've seen the signs of the end, they are lying to you. Jesus also said those days would be exactly like the days of Noah and Lot. No warning!

The people of Noah's day didn't know the end was coming. There were no signs, no warnings - it was just 'business as usual' until the flood came and swept the wicked away.

For in the days before the flood, people were eating and drinking, marrying and giving in marriage, up to the day Noah entered the ark. And they were oblivious until the flood came and swept them all away. So will it be at the coming of the Son of Man. (Matt.24:38-39)

The people of Lot's day didn't know the end was coming. There were no signs, no warnings - it was just 'business as usual' until fire came down from heaven and consumed the wicked.

In the days of Lot, people were eating and drinking, buying and selling, planting and building. But on the day Lot left Sodom, fire and sulfur rained down from heaven and destroyed them all. It will be just like that on the day the Son of Man is revealed. (Lk 17:28-29)

Jesus taught that everything will seem normal right up to the last day of existence on this earth. There will be no signs, no warnings - it will be just 'business as usual' until Jesus returns and the wicked are suddenly 'taken' to destruction.

People were eating, drinking, buying and selling, planting and building, marrying and being given in marriage up until the time of destruction. It will be just like this on the day the Son of Man is revealed. (Luke 17:26-30)

Scriptures' teaching shows the end will not happen during a time of war or upheaval but during a time of peace when people feel secure and things seem to be going well.

For when they say, 'peace and safety', sudden destruction will come upon them, and they will not escape. (1 Thes.5:3)

Why do we listen to those who point to imaginary 'signs' of the end? Every generation has new 'prophets' shouting about some new sign that they believe points to the end of the world. They have been consistently wrong for over 2000 years!

Jesus told us not to follow them! There will be no signs of his return for the world to see! It will be 'business as usual' halted by sudden destruction!

No new signs!

Jesus expressly warned us not to look for signs because he, himself, is 'the sign' God promised to give the people of the world before the last day arrives. He is the only sign God has approved.

Jesus said, 'an evil generation seeks after a sign, but no sign will be given to it, except the sign of Jonah. For as Jonah was a sign to the Ninevites, so the Son of Man will be a sign to this generation'. (Lk.11:29)

Jesus is the last sign!

Most people know the story of Jonah, who was swallowed by a 'big fish'. He spent three days and nights in the belly of that fish before taking salvation to Nineveh. Likewise, Jesus spent three days and nights in the belly of the earth before releasing his Spirit on the saved.

Jesus' mighty, sign-filled death and resurrection, combined with the dramatic 'fire' and 'wind' coming of the Spirit at Pentecost, made up God's final spectacular sign to the world. Finally, his promised last days, filled with the new Laws and a New Covenant that would bring eternal life, had begun.

There will be no more signs!

No warning!

When Jesus finally returns, his arrival will be sudden. On a day when everything is 'business as usual', like lightning, he will suddenly appear. That means people of all nationalities will be buying and selling, marrying and giving in marriage, building and planting, eating and drinking, working and sleeping, right up until the last day of human history.

When he returns, it will be in blazing fire with his powerful angels, and the might of his majesty will be unmistakable. He will destroy the wicked with the breath of his mouth and then gather his 'faithful' and raise them to eternal glory.

- There won't be any warning!
- People won't have time to repent!

On that day, many will find out, too late, that Christ is supreme Lord over all. That he is who he said he was and will do what he said he would do!

> At the name of Jesus, every knee shall bow, in heaven and on earth, and under the earth, and every tongue confess that Jesus Christ is Lord, to the glory of the Father. (Phil.2:9-11)

Many false prophets who tell us to look for a sign also tell us that Jesus, when he returns, will set himself up in the temple in Jerusalem and rule over this current world with his faithful followers - though how that would work, they can't explain.

See for yourself what Scripture says will happen to the earth when Christ returns. What do you think?

A voice from heaven cried, "It is done!" Then there came flashes of lightning, rumblings, peals of thunder and a severe earthquake. No earthquake like it has ever occurred since the beginning of time, so tremendous was the quake.

Jerusalem split into three parts, and all the cities of the nations collapsed. Every island fled away, and the mountains disappeared.

From the sky, huge hailstones, each weighing about a hundred pounds, fell onto people. (Rev.16:18-21)

The sun became dark, and the moon turned red as blood. Then the stars of the sky fell to the earth like figs falling from a tree shaken by a strong wind.

The heavens receded like a scroll being rolled up, and every mountain and island was removed from its place.

The kings of the earth, the princes, the generals, the rich, the mighty, and everyone else hid in caves and among the rocks of the mountains. And they cried to the mountains and the rocks, "Fall on us and hide us from the face of the one who sits on the throne and from the wrath of the Lamb." (Rev.6:12-16)

When talking about the return of Christ, the Apostle Peter said the same things as both Apostles Paul and John. The 'Day of the Lord', the day when Christ returns, is a day from which this earth will never recover.

> *The heavens will disappear with a roar; the elements will melt in the heat and be destroyed by fire, and the earth and everything done in it will be laid bare. (2 Pet.3:10)*

These images are cataclysmic!

It's clear that what is being described is the end of the world. This is what will happen when Christ returns! No one can survive beyond this point.

There are no mountains left on the earth, and all the islands have sunk into the sea. Every city on the planet, both large and small, is totally destroyed, the ground is melted like lava, and there is no more sky or atmosphere - no air.

- There are no cities left to rule.
- There are no people left to rule over.
- The earth is no longer habitable.

Instead of following people seeking signs and making up stories, maybe we should be following 'the sign' himself and seeking ways to be found faithfully keeping his commands when he returns!

He is the only sign we need!

We've seen what
the Book of Revelation
doesn't teach,
so now let's look
at what it does teach!

THE TRUTH IS A DELIGHTFUL SURPRISE

CHAPTER 10

If 'end-times'
is a myth,
then what is
Revelation
really about?

UNVEILED GLORY

Now that we've explored what the Book of Revelation doesn't teach, let's take a look at what that wonderful book does teach.

The name itself gives us a big clue. It is called 'The Revelation of Jesus Christ'. 'Revelation' means 'unveiling'. So the title tells us this book is written to unveil the glory and authority Christ received after he was raised from the dead.

It's about Jesus!

The Book of Revelation is not hard to understand. It's not difficult to read. It's a book with a story, and like any other book, the story it holds has a beginning, a middle and an end.

There are only twenty-two very short chapters in total, so it doesn't take long to read Revelation, and the plot is easy to follow.

Yes! Easy!

So many gruesome tales have been told about this glorious book it has been put by many into the 'too-hard basket' and left virtually unread, but I encourage you to take it out and read it.

It's not as daunting as it seems, particularly when you follow the plot. Yes, Revelation has a very easy-to-follow plot, which hasn't changed since it was penned by the Apostle John over 2000 years ago.

Let me give you a glimpse...

As I mentioned, there are only twenty-two reasonably short chapters in the Book of Revelation, and when they are laid out side by side and looked at from a writer's point of view, the 'plot' of the entire book becomes easy to see.

A plot is like a guideline which holds everything written in place. Writers use the plot as a reference to eliminate anything which deviates from the intended message of the story.

So, when we lay out all the chapters of Revelation and look at the plot running through the entire storyline, it becomes easy to see what has been 'added' and is, therefore, out of place.

Glaringly obvious!

For example, a human Antichrist, ruler over the nations, doesn't fit the original plot, and so to 'add' it, the plot has to be adjusted. In other words, every reference to Christ being made ruler over the nations must be removed and the plot altered in order for this addition to fit the new storyline.

It's the same with the Rapture Theory. In order to add it, the plot needs to be altered. This means that for the Rapture to happen before the 'supposed' tribulation starts, Jesus and his Bride would have to be removed from the story prior to the beginning of the action chapters. The trouble with that is, once you remove Jesus and his Bride, the story stops.

For every addition, there is a subtraction. It's the same with all the 'additions' to the Book of Revelation. To add them, something else needs to be altered or taken out.

In effect, every single time a new 'addition' to Revelation is presented, another part of Revelation must be 'taken out' in order for the new story to make any sense.

And confusion reigns!

It's no wonder that the majority of Christians don't want to read the Book Revelation for themselves anymore. So many conflicting ideas have been added to Revelation that what is actually written now no longer reflects what people expect to read.

Instead of reading with joy and feeling blessed, they close the book feeling confused and think the problem must be their own lack of understanding. It's not! It's those unholy additions!

The truth is simple!

The pure and simple truth is that Revelation is about Jesus. There is nothing in his wonderful Testimony that is scary or frightening. It was written to give his Bride hope, encouragement and the promise of an eternally happy future.

I mentioned the plot of Revelation. Let me just lay it out for you the way it was written over 2000 years ago. You will be surprised at what you see.

I haven't changed anything!

Please bear in mind that I haven't changed this plot. This is the order of events written by John in Revelation. When all the hype is removed, and the chapters are laid out side by side, it is easy to see the overall story and message. This is what we see.

CHAPTER 1: The Royal Decree

In the first chapter, God, Christ and the Seven Spirits introduce themselves as the authors of this work and nominate John as their appointed scribe to write down what they show him. Christ confirms to John that this story is His testimony, the story of His life.

CHAPTERS 2-3: The Royal Bride

The royal 'bride-to-be' is introduced as a person of position and authority who needs protection and guidance in order to remain safe. She is warned of seven plots against her, and seven agents of the Kingdom are sent to keep her safe.

CHAPTERS 4-7: Back At The Palace

The lavish splendour of the vast Kingdom of the ancient King is revealed as we are taken to the throne room, where we find the King waiting for his Son to return from his battle at Calvary. The Son arrives, is crowned as the victor and begins His rule as King by taking immediate action, with His Father's full support, to bring an end to all enemy-inspired insurrections within the Kingdom.

CHAPTERS 8-16: The New King Goes To War

All the enemies of the Kingdom, the vicious dragon, his two ugly beasts, three deceiving frogs and the dragon's wicked queen, are either destroyed or permanently imprisoned during this time. But one enemy stands out more than the others, and she is given cameo treatment.

CHAPTERS 17-20: The Wicked Queen

As the cameo expands, we see the Great Whore of Babylon, the wicked queen, a master at seducing the innocent with trickery, deception and bribes, being given special attention in four chapters. Who she is, what she has done, how she has done it, her partners in crime and their combined final demise are all recorded in these chapters. Just before this wicked queen dies, the young King calls his beloved to *'come away from her'* so she will not be hurt when the wicked queen falls to her death.

CHAPTERS 21-22: The Royal Marriage

The joy in the Kingdom at the return of the victorious hero, the beauty of his bride, their lavish marriage and 'happy-ever-after' future are all described in these two final chapters.

Does this plot sound familiar?

The plot of Revelation, in its most simple form, has been understood and loved for centuries. It is the basis of the fairytale genre.

Many people say the Bible is a fairytale, but the reality is the other way around. Fairytales only exist because of the amazing story of salvation!

Christ is the bravest, most loving and selfless royal hero who ever lived.

All the fairytales about the profound love of a royal hero who fights beasts and slays dragons for a damsel in distress are based on Christ's story, the story of Salvation, recorded as the Gospel.

That the hero takes his rescued bride-to-be to his kingdom, where they marry and live happily-ever-after, reflects the sure hope of our salvation explained so beautifully for the redeemed in the Book of Revelation.

An unchanging plot!

This way of looking at Revelation is not new doctrine! This is old doctrine! The unchanging plot of the Book of Revelation has been known, loved and shared this way for centuries.

Before the printing press was invented and books were freely available, the message of the Gospel was passed from generation to generation through stories even children could understand.

It's all about love!

In its simplest form, that's what the Book of Revelation has always been about! It is the greatest love story ever told! There will never be any greater!

The royal hero who defeats a vicious dragon, two ugly beasts, three deceiving frogs and a thoroughly wicked queen, showers those who join him in his battle against evil with riches beyond measure. And, in the end, everyone lives happily-ever-after.

That is not a scarytale!
Nor is it a fairytale!

The truth about Revelation is not frightening; it is glorious - and easy to remember! It contains the most comforting, encouraging promise of hope any believer can ever read. The whole book exists to show how God places all the enemies of Christ under his feet. And that's exactly what happens.

Every single judgment that flows out from the Scroll of Judgment in Christ's hands is aimed at Satan and his followers. None of them falls on the redeemed! All the so-called havoc that Satan and his Antichrist world ruler are supposed to wield on Earth are, in reality, the curses God has spoken against Satan to destroy his influence on Earth forever.

Judgment is in Christ's hands!

Revelation shows us clearly that Satan does not have the authority to judge. *That is Jesus' role!* He does not hold the Scroll of Judgment or call forth the Four mighty Horsemen to bring judgment. *That is Jesus' role!* He does not separate the sheep from the goats. *That is Jesus' role!* He cannot 'mark' people for judgment. *That, too, is Jesus' role.*

Satan is not all-powerful. He is only an angel and a defeated angel at that! He can never stop people from receiving the 'mark' of Salvation. And he cannot order Christ's mark of Salvation to be removed from the redeemed. Hallelujah!

Not so long ago, the church used to recognise and rejoice in the might of Christ. Christians used to sing about his sovereign role in judgment with gusto. Do you remember this hymn? Read the words; they are straight out of Revelation...

Mine Eyes Have Seen the Glory
(By Mrs Julia Ward Howe)

Mine eyes hath seen the glory
    of the coming of the Lord;
He is trampling out the vintage
    where the grapes of wrath are stored;
He hath loosed the fateful lightning
    of His terrible swift sword;
His truth is marching on.

Glory! Glory! Hallelujah!
Glory! Glory! Hallelujah!
Glory! Glory! Hallelujah!
His truth is marching on.

He has sounded forth the trumpet
    that shall never call retreat;
He is sifting out the hearts of men
    before His judgment seat;
Oh, be swift, my soul, to answer Him!
    Be jubilant, my feet;
Our God is marching on.

This triumphal hymn reflects what Christians used to believe before Godless and destructive 'end-time' teaching gave Christ's role in judgment to Satan.

Flee from that unholy lie!

There are so many beautiful things to explore in the Book of Revelation. The layers of Christ's revealed glory are breathtaking! For instance:

- *How does Revelation explain the meaning of Christ's title, 'Alpha and Omega'? It does!*
- *How does the 'Bride' rule and reign with Christ in Revelation? She does!*
- *Who are the three frogs who lead all the kings of the world to Armageddon? They do!*
- *How does the number 666 reveal Christ's victory over Satan? It does!*
- *Who do the 'four living creatures' around the throne represent? The answer is there!*
- *What control do the 'four living creatures' have over the four horsemen? Surprising!*
- *Why do the seven Spirits of God adorn Christ like a crown when he appears on the throne?*
- *What are the seven names of those Spirits? Are they found in the New Testament? Yes!*
- *What are the seven royal rewards offered to all the redeemed who overcome? Can we know?*
- *What does the Bride do while Christ brings about the end of life on earth? Another surprise!*

There is no need for any believer to fear Satan, his beasts, his wicked queen or his demonic spirits. Like Christ, we overcome everything Satan can throw at us by the blood of the Lamb, by the word of our testimony about his victory at Calvary and by loving him more than our own earthly lives.

We actually can't lose!

For those who believe the lie, straight from Satan, that Christianity is on the decline and will likely be wiped out by this latest Satanic scheme, let me point to something in Revelation which proves categorically that Christianity is not on the decline and Christians will never be wiped out.

> *They gathered all the rulers and their armies to a place with the Hebrew name Armageddon. (Rev.16:16)*
>
> *Then I saw the beast and the kings of the earth with their armies assembled to wage war. (Rev.19.19)*
>
> *And they marched up over the breadth of the earth and encircled the camp of the saints. But fire came down out of heaven and devoured them. (Rev.20:8-9)*

These Scriptures show, without any shadow of doubt, that Christians, as a group, are so large and powerful on the Earth at the time Christ returns that ALL the nations must join together just to have the numbers to surround us. We are mighty in number!

They can't win!

Think about it! Every nation on earth must join forces to become large enough in number to surround the saints. This is overwhelming proof that, even before Armageddon, every other attempt to destroy us and our faith in Christ and halt our influence in the world has failed miserably. Wow!

God is in control!

Though Satan and his agents stir up the antichrists within the nations and gather them together to destroy God's people, they don't realise they are playing right into God's hands. God is actually using their hatred of us to muster *them* into a place where *they* can be destroyed by him.

I have decided to assemble the nations, to gather the Kingdoms and pour out my wrath on them - all my fierce anger. The whole world will be consumed by the fire of my jealous anger. (Zeph.3:9)

Satan and his followers don't know that God is always in control. Even with all the advertising God has done and the book he has written about their demise, they still don't see him coming.

They proudly continue to believe they alone are in God-like control of the events on Earth. Won't they be cranky when they find out they're not? Revelation shows what God will do to them when they are finally able to surround us. It's not pretty!

These Scriptures are incredibly encouraging! What a blessing to know in advance how things will work out for the redeemed! All we need to remember to do now is 'hold the line'!

That's why Revelation was written; to encourage us so that we will have the strength to stand even when surrounded by the enemy!

Let's get back to the truth!

Spiritually, end-time mythology is a trap set up by Satan to get us to take our eyes off Christ and put them onto him instead. That's the only way he can gain worship. Flee from that wickedness!

Practically, end-time mythology is part of a current political ploy to introduce false doctrine as an opiate to immobilise Christians so that Satan's servants can attempt, once again, to rule the world on his behalf. Will they succeed? No! They don't stand a chance.

> *Jesus said to them. "All authority in Heaven and on Earth has been given to me." (Matt.28:18)*

> *Great and marvellous are your deeds, Lord God Almighty. Just and true are your ways, King of the nations. Who will not fear you, Lord, and bring glory to your name? (Rev.15:3-4)*

And God's people said 'Amen'!

Who would dare use
false doctrine
as an opiate
to muzzle and control
Christ's redeemed?

DECEPTION TRAVELS ACROSS TIME

CHAPTER 11

When did this great end-time deception begin? Does anyone know?

AN EFFECTIVE MUZZLE

Christ is King over all kings and Lord over all lords. He is the ruler of the Earth, and all demons and spiritual forces must submit to his authority. There is not one demon who can withstand his command, and that includes Satan.

> *The disciples said with joy, "Lord, even the demons submit to us in Your name." So Jesus told them, "I saw Satan fall like lightning from Heaven. I have given you authority to tread on serpents and scorpions, and over all the power of the enemy, and nothing shall hurt you. (Luke 10:17-19)*

This is the authority of Christ. This is the authority he has passed on to all his redeemed. So, why are we not using our authority? Why are we standing back and allowing wickedness to flourish?

Have you ever wondered why the body of Christ is quiet on important social matters? Why the church is not speaking up? Why God's people are no longer actively working for change?

Despite the fact that Christianity in 2022 was the largest and most influential group in the world, with over 2.56 billion people out of a 7.8 billion world population (31% of all people on the planet), we have remained silent as evil grows and swirls around us. Why is this?

It wasn't always that way!

Christian values and the democracy they built and nurtured are being torn down piece by piece. And we are sitting on our hands and letting it happen! Why are we remaining quiet?

We still have the power to turn the world upside down. And now, more than ever, we have the numbers to do it, and yet we don't speak out.

> *You Christians look after a document containing enough dynamite to blow all civilization to pieces, turn the world upside down and bring peace to a battle-torn planet. But you treat it as though it is nothing more than a piece of literature. (Mahatma Gandhi)*

Was Mahatma Gandhi right?

Could the lack of Christian social action be tied to our theological viewpoint? Could the lawlessness and disrespect for God's ways currently taking over Western society be linked to modern 'end-time' theology'? Have we been taught to turn a blind eye and let the evil happen?

I believe we have!

By the early 1960s, a theological movement that became known as 'the death of God' had risen to prominence in America. Its rise led to that famous *Time Magazine* headline of 1966, "God is dead!"

146

Around the same time, a new teaching started to infiltrate the church. It was catapulted into the minds of Christians through a young musician, Larry Norman, who wrote and performed the infamous song *"I Wish We'd All Been Ready"*.

The tenets of that song and the new theology behind it became the basis of the *Left Behind* series of books by Tim La Haye and Jerry B Jenkins, which were later immortalised in a series of films, the last of which was released in 2014.

Decades of false teaching!

Songs, visual media, a raft of supportive Hollywood movies, rapid changes in the world's understanding of a single antichrist person, and even grammatical changes in spell-checkers forcing us to capitalise 'antichrist' and singularise the word by adding 'the' in front each time it's used, have all contributed to the rise and rapid acceptance of this new, world-approved, 'end-time' mythology.

Over sixty to seventy years, a whole generation of Christians has been taught to believe that Satan has replaced God in all the ways that matter. The new and readily acceptable 'end-time' theology shows God as impotent, far away, and unable to stop the supposedly more powerful Satan from doing whatever he wants in the world. In effect, even in the church, God may as well be dead!

"And they worshipped the beast!"

How did these heretical ideas enter the church? How did they take hold so quickly? Did these false teachings arise by accident, or were they deliberately insinuated into Christian doctrine? Were they an attempt to manipulate the Christian population?

It's been done before...

Emporer Constantine, AD 306-337, overtook the true religion set up by Christ and used it to smooth the way for his political domination of the Roman Empire. He changed the doctrine, included pagan traditions, decreed it to be the new 'universal' world religion (Catholicism) and set it up by force, persecuting the real Christians who resisted. He used his new religion to gain control of the people.

In the same way, the recent dumbing-down of Christians in the West is a planned political ploy to keep the massive Christian population subdued and quiet as a new social order is introduced. Changing the doctrine is seen as a way of gaining control over people, and it works. It simply requires the planting of false prophets to teach the new doctrine.

An old and common tactic!

Way back in history, a prophet called Balaam advised King Balak to do the same thing to the Israelites, again for political reasons. Balak took Balaam's advice, and it worked for a time until God punished the Israelites to get them back on track. Let's look at the story...

Balaam and Balak
(Numbers 22-25)

King Balak wanted to conquer the Israelites. They were great in number, and he would not have been able to overtake them by force.

So he hired the prophet Balaam, who advised him that they were powerfully protected by their God, the God of Israel, and couldn't be overcome while they remained obedient to him and kept all his commandments.

In response to this information, Balak launched a subtle attack on their obedience in order to weaken their relationship with their powerful God so that they would lose his protection, become weak and be easily overthrown.

Balak planted seductive temple prostitutes who added pagan doctrines and rituals into their usual worship routines.

Using interesting variety and attractive religious distractions, Balak deceived God's people into disobeying his word, successfully weakening their relationship with him. God punished his people by sending a sudden plague, which killed 24,000 in a short time.

Thankfully, Moses and a few other Godly men could see what was happening, and because of their prayers and swift actions to rid Israel of the introduced Baal worship, the plague was halted, and Balak's plans were thwarted.

Jesus warned us about this...

Yet you have some among you who hold to the teaching of Balaam who taught Balak to entice my people to sin... Repent! (Rev.2:12-17)

In one of his seven letters in Revelation, Jesus warns us that not rebuking false doctrine in the churches will lead to sin and the desolation it brings.

Is this what is happening in Western churches? I believe it is! Is it deliberate? I believe it is! Are God's people being subtly enticed into sin? I believe we are. And you might be surprised at the source!

Nothing is easier than to give Christian asceticism a socialist tinge. (Karl Marx - Manifesto of the Communist Party,1848)

Karl Marx wrote those chilling words more than a century ago. And he proved it could be done. *Love your neighbour* became '*for the good of the people*' and '*for the good of the party*'. He had no problem giving Christian doctrine a '*socialist tinge.*'

Today, Communism *per se*, like Balak's armies, would have been easy for today's Christians to see and reject. Its motives are out there in plain sight. Christians would not have fallen for communist lies, and our resistance would have defeated them. No! Subtlety was needed, and subtlety was achieved.

The New World Order

During WWII, the tenets of the *'Communist Manifesto'* were skilfully reworded and woven into a global action plan by the UN and UNESCO and published as an established political aim just before this tsunami of false teaching began.

The moral for UNESCO is clear. It must envisage some form of world political unity - **a single world government** *or otherwise...and familiarize all peoples with the implications of* **the transfer of full sovereignty** *from separate nations to a world organization. (UNESCO Charter, 1946)*

UNESCO (the UN's education program) was set up by a man named Julian Huxley, who came from a family of Darwinists - firm believers in eugenics. He was an enthusiastic advocate of depopulation and robotics and coined the word 'transhumanism'.

His brother, Aldous Huxley, wrote the famous dystopian novel *Brave New World* and mentored George Orwell in 1948 as he wrote the extremely disturbing novel *1984. (See notes ** in 'More Info')*

Far worse than Communism!

If Communists alone had suddenly sprung on us the horrific concept of the transfer of full sovereignty of our nation to an unelected, unaccountable single-world-dictatorship and the destruction of all Christian beliefs, there would have been an uproar.

But today, there's no uproar!

Karl Marx's comrades have no conscience about infiltrating churches and altering the Gospel to fulfil their political ambitions. *"Nothing is easier!"* Now we find that today's Christians have been so brainwashed by false doctrine over the last sixty to seventy years that in seeing a dystopian-style one-world government emerge, we don't even blink.

A one-world government and a new Godless world order, the communist dream, are now mixed with Globalism, LGBTI, Climate Alarmism, Cancel Culture, Abortions, Euthanasia, Sexualisation of Children, Depopulation, Bio Weapons, Pandemic Treaties, Racism, Digital Identity, Microchip Implants, Food Shortages and the tearing down of morality, traditions, history and national sovereignty. This is far worse than Communism alone could ever be!

Heavily disguised as 'good'!

Communist rhetoric has been freely used during the pandemic. Forced vaccinations are presented as being '*good for others*'. Forced green energy is touted as '*good for the world*'. Forced acceptance of mass murder and the sexualisation of children is presented as being '*good for society*'. In Australia, division by race is now being promoted as '*good for the country*'. Those who disagree are called 'selfish'. Once again, '*Love your neighbour*' has been successfully twisted out of context, given '*a socialist tinge*' and presented to the world as the 'new normal', the New World Order.

Communism on Steroids!

Without a doubt, the greatest threat to the establishment of this vile totalitarian utopia is the Christian population! We are billions and have both natural and supernatural power to stop the above from happening. Yet we are not saying a word! Where is the outcry from Christian leadership? There has not been a peep!

What are we doing?

Our enemies, the UN | UNESCO | WHO | WEF, and the small group of 'elites' they serve, are very cunning. We are too large a group for them to overtake by force. They must weaken our faith, our resolve and our resistance to their plans. Like Balak, they are diabolically patient as they wait for us to yield. And like the Israelites, we now find we have false teachers in our midst, supporting the new *'socialist'* normal. Their 'end-time' doctrine is merely a tool to encourage us to become so familiar with the idea of a dystopian-style one-world-government that when it appears, there will be no surprise, no outcry and most importantly, no resistance.

The opiate of the people!

This deadly new 'end-time' doctrine has been shockingly effective at silencing us. Because of the 'single Antichrist' myth, most Christians have their eyes fixed on the horizon. And while we are looking for a single antichrist leader to show up, we don't even notice the many antichrists systematically tearing us, our families, our culture, our values, our nations and the world apart.

Using doctrine to control people is easy for false prophets and teachers to do, as it has long been common practice for paid ministry to use their influence to keep the Christian population subdued and obedient to changing government policies.

> *We have used the Bible as if it were a mere policeman's handbook, an opium dose for keeping beasts of burden patient while they were being overloaded, a mere book to keep the poor in order. (Charles Kingsley. Canon of the Church of England, 1847)*

During the pandemic, many church leaders have been openly paid or subtly bribed to keep Christians subdued and quiet so that we won't speak out against the ravaging of our morals, principles and freedoms. This 'control through doctrine' is the teaching of Balaam that Jesus warned us about! He demands rebuke and repentance!

So, what do we do?

False prophets and teachers come in all different shapes and sizes and are present in every gathering of believers. Despite popular belief, they fill many pulpits, yet they all have one thing in common; they all *speak like a dragon*. Their teaching is their 'fruit'.

Jesus put the onus on each one of us to sort out who is true and who is false. He told us to judge those who are teaching us. He told us he expects us to be able to recognise false prophets by their fruit.

Beware of false prophets. They come to you in sheep's clothing, but inwardly, they are ravenous wolves. By their fruit, you will recognise them. (Matt.7:15-16)

From the fruit of his mouth, a man's heart is filled, and with the harvest of his lips, he is satisfied. (Prov.18:20-21)

When the heretical lies are pointed out and highlighted, it becomes easy to see who is speaking truth and who is deceiving the elect.

A simple comparison!

The true Bible-based Gospel: Jesus ushered in the last days (Heb.1:1-2). Jesus is God's only named and appointed last days ruler over all the kings of the earth (Rev.1:15). Jesus has overcome tribulation (Jn.16:33). Jesus has commissioned his followers to go into the world and preach the Gospel (Matt.28:18-20). Jesus will return on the last day (Jn.6:40).

The fake end-time gospel: The last days will begin sometime in the near future (No verse / Nothing about Jesus). At that time, Satan will rule the nations through his human Antichrist world leader (No verse / Nothing about Jesus). Tribulation will be unbearable (No verse / Nothing about Jesus). Since the Gospel has already been preached to all nations (No verse / No great commission), there is nothing for Christians to do but hunker down and dodge evil while awaiting a 'pre' last day rapture (No verses anywhere).

If we or an angel from heaven should preach a gospel contrary to the one we preached to you, let him be under a divine curse. (Gal.1:8)

The false and pointedly socialist 'end-time' theology is the kind of 'other gospel' Paul was warning us about. It is poisoned fruit!

Nevertheless, with constant false teaching coming from more and more pulpits and books, many Christians began to believe that fighting the futuristic 'last days' evil was pointless. "It was prophesied, wasn't it?" "Opposing it is like opposing God's will; better to just wait for Christ to return".

Christians stopped fighting evil!

The church fell asleep to the sound of many false prophets and deceivers, smoothly claiming Christ had sent them when he had not and filling their heads with plausible lies which, in effect, paralysed their walk and left them unable to do the stated will of God. Yet, Christ warned us they would come:

Many false prophets will arise and mislead many. Because of the multiplication of wickedness, the love of most (for God) will grow cold. But those who endure to the end will be saved. And this gospel of the kingdom will be preached in all the world as a testimony to all nations, and then the end will come. (Matt.24:13)

The false and blasphemous 'end-time' teaching, which encourages everyone to endure the evil they see in the world around them while they wait for Christ to come and rapture them away, is preventing God's people from doing the only thing Jesus said will hasten his return.

Christ said he would return only after the church had boldly preached the Gospel in all nations. Is that happening in our nation? In other Western nations?

Teach them to obey all that I have commanded you. I am with you always, even to the end of the age. (Matt.28:20)

The preaching of the Gospel is the will of God! It is the command of Christ. It is the role of the church! Yet, it's not happening! You can't preach to the world while sitting in a pew.

Western nations are now filled with Christians who won't speak up on moral or political issues. They won't stand up for righteousness!

The evil in Western nations keeps growing and taking root because Christians will not stand against the evil they see and will not lobby for Godly Kingdom principles to be upheld in the corridors of power.

Our enemy is counting on us to do nothing. If we stand up against their schemes, they will fail! No 'ifs or buts'; *they will fail!* That's why they have put so much effort into trying to deceive us. We have the numbers and the power to stop them in their tracks!

Apathy is poison!

Christians make up sixty per cent of our population in Australia. We should not have a problem with abortion, euthanasia or transgender education in our schools. We should not have a problem saying 'No!' loud and clear to the WHO's medical coercion and communist-style control. But we do have a problem! Why? Because Christians believe the lie that evil has to happen. No, it doesn't!

Evil is what we need to fight!

It's clear from the Apostle Paul's teaching in 2Thes.2:10-12 that God is watching to see who loves the truth enough to reject the great lie. And he explains that the truth is found in the preaching of the true Gospel.

Anyone who believes the outrageous lie that evil is God's will does not understand the truth of the Gospel. The purpose of the Cross was to overcome evil, and Jesus died so that we, like him, could overcome evil with good. After he was raised from the dead, Christ had the Book of Revelation written to teach us how to overcome Satan, the two beasts and the whore, in the same way he overcame them.

We are on the winning team!

It's time to show Western society that God is not dead and the Gospel of Christ is still the power of God for salvation to everyone who believes.

Scripture compels us to act!

The reason the Son of God appeared was to destroy the devil's work. (1John 3:8)

Do not be overcome by evil, but overcome evil with good. (Rom.12.21)

Resist the devil, and he will flee from you. (James 4:7)

We demolish arguments and every pretension that sets itself up against the knowledge of God, and we take captive every thought to make it obedient to Christ. (2 Cor.10:3-5)

Truly, I tell you, whatever you bind on earth will be bound in heaven, and whatever you loose on earth will be loosed in heaven. (Matt.18:18)

And if two of you on earth agree about anything they ask for, it will be done for them by my Father in heaven. (Matt.18:19)

In all these things, we are more than conquerors through Him who loved us. (Rom.8:37)

No weapon that is formed against you will prosper, and every tongue that accuses you in judgment you will condemn. (Is.54:17)

I will build my church, and the gates of hell shall not prevail against it. (Matt.16:18)

What, then, shall we say to these things? If God is for us, who is against us? (Rom.8:31)

We must resist evil!

These powerful Scriptures (and there are many more) show the will of God and the heart of God regarding evil. It is clear we need to stand against evil, resist it, condemn it, tear it down, destroy it, overcome it, conquer it, bind it and bring it captive to the will of God.

Fighting evil is God's will. It has always been his will. The entire history of the Bible reveals the rock-solid and obvious truth that God does not, and never will, approve of evil. He is holy, and evil is unholy.

I am the LORD your God; consecrate yourselves, therefore, and be holy because I am holy. (Lev.11:33)

Be holy, as I am holy!

Overcoming evil is what is required of those who say they love God, Christ and the truth. This is what separates the sheep from the goats. True Christians can never be Christians in name only; we must be holy! And we can only be holy if we stand in God's camp and shun everything evil.

If we are not actively doing the will of God by openly resisting, tearing down and overcoming the things God says are evil, we are not being his salt, shining his light or taking his love to the world. We are asleep. We have swallowed the opiate, the end-time lie that Satan is more powerful than God, and we are deceived. It's time to wake up!

Take a good look
at what is
happening
all over the world!

THIS CURRENT EVIL HAS BECOME GLOBAL

CHAPTER 12

When evil
grows like a cancer,
it's time for
drastic action!

CUT IT OUT

Why are democratic governments all around the world falling for the UN | UNESCO | WHO | WEF propaganda? Why are they tearing down their own traditions, constitutions, and cultures? Why are they promoting the *Great Reset* and *New World Order* as the *New Normal*? It is the stuff of despots!

Those flashy new titles are just fancy names for yet another antiquated 'rich ruling the poor' or 'feudal lord' scenario, where a select handful of wealthy and unaccountable tyrants decide they should rule over the rest of us. For some reason, the elites seem to be operating under the delusion that everyone in the world (and the world itself) belongs to them.

Is that what's happening?

Currently, a mere 1000 wealthy business and political leaders who make up the membership of the World Economic Forum (WEF) are trying to assimilate the world's eight billion people into their new 'universal' world order. A world where they will rule over us with unfettered autonomy, where they will own everything, and we will own nothing. A world where we will be happy - or else!

They are telling us we need this *Great Reset,* this *Brave New World*, this distorted, dystopian *New World Order* because the *Current World Order* doesn't work any more. This begs an obvious question...

Who runs the current world order?

Oh, that's right, the same people who now tell us it doesn't work! The players haven't changed. They are still the same as they have been for decades.

- The same people who are in the position to end world hunger and poverty immediately! Right now! Today! But won't!

- The same people who provoke wars and finance armaments to grow their wealth and brag about their 'power'.

- The same people who broker the destruction of nations in order to gain from rebuilding.

- The same people who pay for the development of biochemical weapons and profit from selling the antidote.

- The same people who invented destructive 'climate change' ideology to sell their 'green' energy products, which rape the world and do unfixable environmental harm.

- The same people who set up the international banking and global trade systems, which they now tell us are failing.

Why would we listen to the people who have made an obscene amount of money deliberately creating a total mess of this world when they tell us they have developed a new plan and all we have to do is trust them? Trust them with what?

Our entire lives, apparently...

Their new aim is to control every person on the planet. They want to decide where we live, the home we live in, the food we eat, when and if we travel, the work we do, the wages we receive, our sexual partners, the number of children we have and to whom we have them, the medications we take, the thoughts we think, the emotions we feel and, ultimately, the date we must die. They want god-like control over us!

This is called slavery!

They want to monitor their slaves through their new 'digital identity' systems, which are not just about financial transactions but include proposed brain implants to regulate and control our thoughts.

Are their 'digital identity' systems going to make the world a better place? Their track record says NO! They destroy everything they touch! They want to make the world a huge and brutally controlled prison, hence the 15-minute travel zones and 'Smart Cities' plans. *Smart City* is just another name for 'prison'.

In their New World Order, as in *'The Hunger Games'* movies, only the elites will be able to enjoy the pleasurable fruits of 'freedom'. The rest of us will be slaves, living under their heels and squashed like bugs if we try to resist their control.

In this New World Order, so the propaganda tells us, we will own nothing and be happy because we will be living in the 'security' of our own little space.

Is this what we want? If not, we need to actively resist. We must start writing to our governments and demanding they ditch the UN | UNESCO | WHO | WEF programs, agreements and partnerships and retain our sovereign freedoms.

We must cleanse our governments of all the UN | UNESCO | WHO | WEF moles that have been deliberately planted within our governments.

*In 2017, Klaus Schwab boasted to WEF members that the WEF had **'penetrated governments with its global leaders'.***

It was those 'planted' leaders who so willingly subjected their countries to the brutally inhumane, communist-style lockdowns during the 'pandemic'.

We must declare as reprehensible all elected leaders who think joining any UN | UNESCO | WHO | WEF program is a good idea. Such leaders are wolves in sheep's clothing, deliberately planted to overthrow the will of the people. We can say, 'no'!

It's not inevitable!

The dystopian novel '1984' was not, as many have thought, a prophetic glimpse into the future or the inevitable next step in the world's history. It was a warning against totalitarianism. Written just after WW11, it was designed to give people a frightening glimpse into what the world *would* have looked like by 1984 if Hitler had won the war. It was designed to scare people and turn them away from fascism forever.

Despite its original purpose, the extreme tenets outlined in the book are now being used as a roadmap to a totalitarian future by the unelected, unaccountable UN | UNESCO | WHO | WEF 'New World Order' alliance. Will they succeed? No! Their despotic plans are doomed!

There are far too many people in the world for them to control. Earth's population would have to be dramatically culled (the mass murder of billions) via plague (bioweapons), famine (destruction of livestock and farmland) and sword (convenient wars) for those few elites to control the rest of us effectively.

Oh, wait! Isn't that what is happening? Yes, it is! Do you really think that most people will simply sit back and let themselves and their children be killed? No! Once people wake up, it's game over for them.

People are not stupid!

On top of that, the **technology to do everything they have planned has yet to be invented**. And even when it is invented, it won't reach everyone in the world, as less than half the world's population has any access to the internet, and barely 50% have access to a phone. The poor still live in makeshift huts with dirt floors and no electricity. Digital currency? Not for them! What are they going to live on? Or will they be callously forced to starve to death? The reality is that none of these outlandish 'control' plans can be implemented until everyone in the world is connected to the internet. And that's a long way off.

We have time to stop this!

Ordinary people have the power to end this madness before it gets any worse. Simple resistance is powerful! There are a few things we can all do now to stop their control from growing:

- Refuse to be herded into their *Smart Cities*. *(They can't control us if we are all spread out).*
- Turn off the mainstream news media *(the source of their propaganda).*
- Say no to digital IDs *(they can't manipulate our lives without them).*
- Take your money out of the big banks *(invest in banks that don't subscribe to digital IDs).*
- Use cash for purchases *(they can't monitor or make money from cash purchases).*
- Boycott businesses that refuse to take cash *(they will go out of business).*
- Ditch toxic solar energy and electric vehicles *(they are Trojan Horses).*
- Boycott companies supporting the 'green' hoax *(they can't survive without our money).*
- Vote out politicians who support the UN | UNESCO | WHO | WEF programs and agendas.
- Reinvest in family and the Christian traditions that have kept us safe for 1000s of years.
- Read some books *(there are many out there speaking the truth).*

We can stop this!

Should we fight
in the natural?

Doesn't Scripture
say we are
not fighting
flesh and blood?

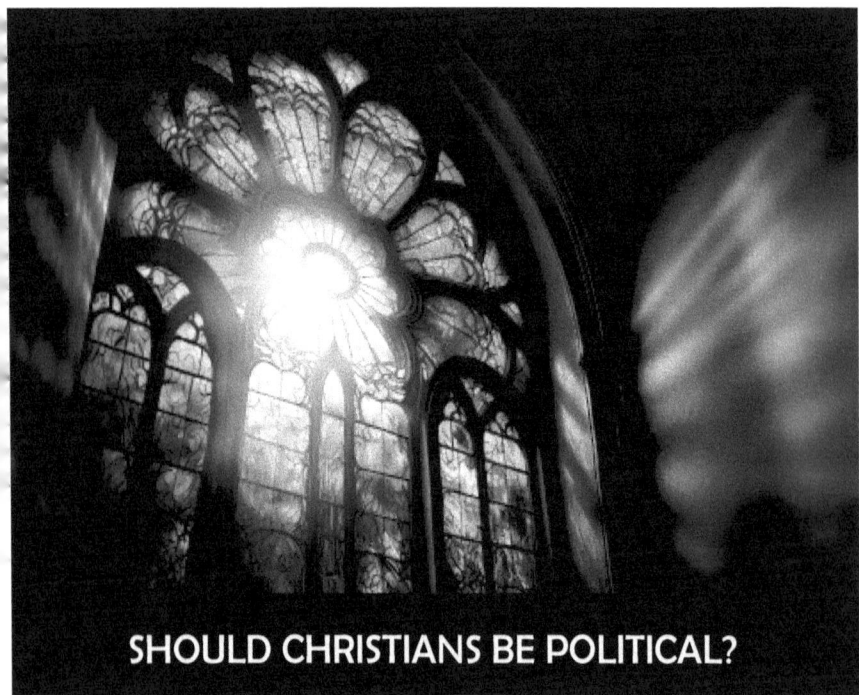
SHOULD CHRISTIANS BE POLITICAL?

CHAPTER 13

Shouldn't we
just pray
and
let God
fight this battle
for us?

CHURCH & STATE

We are not fighting flesh and blood as in hand-to-hand combat, but we are still fighting. We still need to stand for righteousness in an unrighteous world.

One of the lies we have been told is that Christians should not be involved with politics. The so-called 'proof' for that wild assumption is the misquoted *'Division of Church and State'*.

I say misquoted because *'Division of Church and State'* actually means that the government (State) is not allowed to make laws that interfere with Christian (Church) doctrine and practice.

It makes absolutely no sense that a taxpayer would suddenly become ineligible to have an opinion on any political subject the moment they chose to become a Christian. If that was the reality, no Christian would be allowed to vote. Is that the case? Are Christians banned from voting? No!

In Communist countries, the government strictly controls what is taught from pulpits. In free democratic societies, such control is rejected. *'Division of Church and State'* ensures the protection of the church from that kind of government control.

Should we be involved?

So, if Christians are free to be involved in politics, should we be involved? What does the Bible teach?

Nearly all politics!

It may come as a surprise for some to learn that just about everything written in Scripture is political. Let's take a quick look at Biblical history.

Abraham and Lot - political!
When Abraham learned that his nephew Lot had been taken captive by a foreign king, he went to war with the king and freed Lot.

Moses and Pharoah - political!
Everything Moses did, from calling down the ten plagues on Egypt to leading his people through the Red Sea and out of Egypt, was political.

David and Goliath - political!
It is impossible to view David's famous battle with the giant soldier from a foreign army, Goliath, in any other way than as political.

Elijah and Jezebel - political!
Jezebel was a foreign operative in a position of power inside Israel. Every destructive thing she did was political. Her overthrow was political.

Samson and Delilah - political!
The greatest warrior Israel had ever seen, Samson, was deceived by a foreign *femme fatale* planted to find and exploit his weakness.

Deborah and Sisera - political!
The first female ruler of Israel, Deborah, went to war against an enemy nation. Her killing of the notorious Sisera could only be seen as political.

Jonah and the Whale - political!
Jonah was sent by God to offer peace to a violent foreign enemy nation. He didn't want to offer them peace, so he ran. This story is political.

Queen Esther and Haman - political!
The account of Queen Esther's plight, her bravery and the resultant hanging of her enemy, Haman, is political from start to finish.

Jesus and Pilot - political!
Under Roman rule, Jews didn't have any legal rights, so they presented Christ to Pilot as a political threat so that Pilot would have him killed.

Peter's preaching - political!
The early disciples were jailed for preaching. When released, they were forbidden to preach the Gospel. Peter defied that political command.

Paul's imprisonment - political!
Many times in the Book of Acts, Paul was imprisoned for preaching the Gospel. Each court hearing and imprisonment was political.

Armageddon - political!
Just before Christ returns, all the nations of the earth join forces to surround the vast number of Christians in the world. Definitely political!

Bible history is overwhelmingly political! In every Biblical account above (except for Armageddon, as it hasn't happened yet), God abundantly blessed, usually with miracles, those who stood up for righteousness, even the reluctant Jonah.

These accounts (and there are many, many more) show two very important things.

- Firstly, that standing up for God's righteous ways is usually political, and

- Secondly, that standing up for righteousness always includes physical actions that can be seen by others.

People do not light a lamp and put it under a basket. Instead, they set it on a stand, and it gives light to everyone in the house. In the same way, let your light shine before men, that they may see your good deeds and glorify your Father in heaven (Matt.5:16)

Hiding behind words like, *'let's just pray about it'*, or thinking we are doing all we need to do by attending church one day a week is not shining our light. If that's all we do, then that's exactly what is meant by *putting our light under a basket.*

All the patriarchs just listed prayed as well as keeping the Sabbath, but praying and keeping the Sabbath alone would never have produced the miraculous results recorded in Scripture. To see God bring a miraculous result, they had to take physical action. That physical action is called 'faith'.

Despite its common usage, faith is not what we believe. Hope is what we believe but can't yet see. Faith is what we physically do to show our belief. Our actions of faith are the evidence we believe.

Now faith is the substance of things hoped for, the evidence of things not seen. (Heb.11:1)

This is one of the major reasons the church is so weak. There is no emphasis on action! We have been falsely told that faith is what we believe, and that has kept us sitting on our hands. However, the strong evidence of Scripture paints a very different picture of the meaning of faith. Faith is what we do!

So too, faith by itself, if it does not result in action, is dead. (James 2:18)

As the body without the spirit is dead, so faith without action is dead. (James 2.26)

Another Political Account
(2 Sam.15:30-34 - Paraphrased)

King David's son Absalom had decided to take David's kingdom from him by force. When David heard that one of his closest advisers had joined Absalom's rebellion, he became worried.

He knew his ex-adviser, Ahithophel, would give his son a degree of success, so he prayed to God with all sincerity, "Please, Lord, turn his advice into nonsense!"

David knew the nature of God. He knew God had chosen him to be King and would uphold his position as anointed King and not allow anyone, including one of God's own anointed advisors, to rebel against his position.

King David knew he was praying in line with the will of God. He knew God would answer his prayer because he knew the character of God. His hope was sure! But David didn't rest on hope alone. After he prayed, he also took action.

David turned to his other trusted adviser, Hushai, and said, "You can help me now by returning to the city and telling Absalom you will serve him as faithfully as you served his father. Then do all you can to oppose the advice Ahithophel gives."

Hushai did as King David asked, joined Absalom's rebellion, and ultimately found the opportunity to overturn Ahithophel's advice.

As a result, Absalom's plans to kill his father were thwarted. Absalom himself was killed (18:14), and Ahithophel committed suicide (17:23).

King David didn't rely on prayer alone. He took action. He prayed God would 'thwart', and then he sent a skilled advisor to do the 'thwarting'. As soon as King David added visible faith (action) to his invisible hope (prayer), God brought the victory.

A powerful spiritual principle!

King David practised what is termed in the New Testament 'praying in faith'. The principle hasn't changed. Like King David, our prayers live in the area of our sure and firm hope, but it is the action of faith which brings our hope to life and prepares the way for the miracle to happen. We must act!

Miracles require faith!

By Faith, Noah *built* an ark, David *faced* Goliath, Abraham *left his home* and set out to find the promised land, and Moses' parents *broke the law* and hid him from Pharaoh. These were all actions taken before the promised hope they firmly believed and prayed for was actually received.

- Noah believed God's word and acted on it. If he hadn't taken action and built an ark, he would not have seen the miracle of salvation.

- David believed God's word and acted on it. If he hadn't taken the action of challenging Goliath, Israel would not have had the victory.

- Abraham believed God's word and acted on it. If he hadn't taken the action of leaving his home, he would never have entered the promised land.

Jesus encouraged faith!

Jesus encouraged sick people to act in faith. He would give them something to do, and when they obeyed him, they received their miracle. Sometimes, people were already doing actions that allowed Christ to give them a miracle *'because of their faith'*.

- As a blind man *washed* the mud off his eyes, he was healed. (Jn.9:6-7)

- As ten lepers *hurried* to show their diseased skin to the priest, they were healed. (Luke 17:11-14)

- As a woman *touched* the cloak of Christ in faith, she was healed. (Matt.9:20-22)

- When men *lowered* their friend through a roof in faith, he was healed. (Luke 5:17-39)

Each of these miracles, in the Old and New Testaments, needed an action of faith to bring it about. Every action of faith will result in testimony.

An unchanging principle!

Out of our unwavering invisible beliefs flow prayers of hope. Out of our prayers of hope come the visible actions of faith. When these actions of faith are done in obedience to Christ's Law of love, we see astounding miracles, which become mighty testimonies to Christ's glory. So, if we want to overcome by the word of our testimony, we need to:

- Believe that God wants things to change.

- Pray that he will bring change, and then

- Take action to bring about the change.

As we step out in righteous faith, God will step out with us and do the impossible on our behalf. That's what he does. That's his recipe for success.

Will not God bring about justice for His elect who cry out to Him day and night? Will He continue to defer their help? I tell you, He will promptly carry out justice on their behalf. Nevertheless, when the Son of Man comes, will He find faith on the earth? (Luke 18:7-8)

Justice is political!

God is ready to spring into action to bring about justice for his elect, but the big question is, will he be able to? He only takes action when we do. That's why Jesus asked, *"...will He find faith on the earth?"*

When it comes to overcoming evil, Christ has given us a long list of actions we can take and need to take if we want to see God bring the victory.

Resist - In a way that can be seen.

There is nothing passive about this word. It literally means *'exert forceful opposition'* or *'withstand forceful pressure'*.

Resist implies *an overt recognition of a hostile or threatening force and a positive effort to counteract or repel it.* (Merriam-Webster Dictionary)

It's more than simple avoidance or even saying 'no'. It means actively pushing back and repelling the aggressor.

Resist the devil, and he will flee from you. (James 4:7)

Demolish Arguments - Shatter them!

Demolish means *to work, labour or strive to shatter, smash, break to pieces, obliterate and strip of any merit or credence. (Merriam-Webster Dictionary)*

Arguments means *reasons or facts intended to convince or persuade or establish a point of view.* (Merriam-Webster Dictionary)

It's more than just disagreeing with an idea or even saying 'I disagree'. It means presenting truths so well-researched they cannot be refuted.

We demolish arguments and every pretension that sets itself up against the knowledge of God, and we take captive every thought to make it obedient to Christ. (2 Cor.10:3-5)

Condemn - Declare evil as reprehensible.

There may be *no condemnation for those in Christ Jesus,* but obviously, there is condemnation for those who are not part of the Body of Christ. And we are the ones who are supposed to bring that condemnation. Read this verse again.

*No weapon that is formed against you will prosper, and every tongue that accuses you in judgment **you** will condemn. (Is.54:17)*

Condemn means *to declare to be reprehensible, wrong or evil, usually after weighing evidence and without reservation. (Merriam-Webster Dictionary)*

We have the authority from God to declare as reprehensible, wrong or evil anything that sets itself up against the knowledge of God or tries to extinguish Christianity.

'Faith' is not private!

It is clear from these Scriptures that the preaching of the Gospel includes publicly standing against evil, resisting it, condemning it, tearing it down, and bringing it captive to the will of God.

The reason the Son of God appeared was to destroy the devil's work. (1John 3:8)

Do not be overcome by evil, but overcome evil with good. (Rom.12.21)

In all these things, we are more than conquerors through Him who loved us. (Rom.8:37)

What, then, shall we say to these things? If God is for us, who is against us? (Rom.8:31)

We must stop listening to the false prophets who tell us we can't fight Satan and win, or the church is not political, or prayer is enough, or 'faith' is a private matter. Christ came to earth to destroy the works of the devil and teach us how to overcome the evil in the world that Satan and his minions promote.

'The Great Whore' is political!

We know that the Great Whore is the army of people, both male and female, of all tribes, peoples, languages and nations who carry out the plans of the two beasts, whose unchanging purpose is to spread sin and blasphemy throughout the world.

She is responsible for the seduction of wealth, every temptation to immorality, the deaths of everyone murdered or slain - including those killed in war, all slavery and placing a monetary value on every human life (the buying and selling of souls). She proudly boasts of her great wickedness, collecting the evidence of her sin in a golden cup.

The woman was dressed in red and adorned with gold, jewels and pearls. She held in her hand a golden cup full of abominations and the impurities of her sexual immorality.

I could see that the woman was drunk with the blood of the saints and witnesses for Jesus. (Rev.17:4-6)

Can we see her today?

This woman is thoroughly political. The kings and nations drink from her filthy cup. And the merchants of the world grow wealthy through her luxuries. She is seen in the millions of people who support her ways. Can we recognise her work today? Yes!

Like the two beasts, her many works are always focused on tearing down the worship of God and Christ and will always promote the breaking of God's Commandments and the destruction of the powerful testimony of Christ's victory at Calvary. It's easy to see her at work in the world today.

Abortion - breaks God's command.

Tens of millions of babies are killed each year simply because they are not wanted.

You shall not kill a person. (Ex.20:13)

Euthanasia - breaks God's command.

Not just the elderly but the sick, disabled, lonely, homeless and even unwanted children are now being legally 'put down' like animals.

You shall not kill a person. (Ex.20:13)

Depopulation - breaks God's command.

The world is not filled yet. Eight billion people could comfortably fit into one Australian State while the rest of the world remained empty.

Be fruitful and multiply and fill the earth. (Gen.1:28)

Eating Bugs - breaks God's command.

Forced famine, the killing of livestock and the concept of bugs replacing meat as our staple food source is part of the depopulation program.

Do not eat any creature that crawls along the ground. (Lev.11:42)

Sexual Immorality - breaks God's command.

The WHO promoted sexualisation of children in our schools as part of an LBGTI recruitment program is beyond vile. It is detestable.

You shall not commit adultery, which includes sexual immorality, impurity, and lustful sensuality. (Ex.20:14 & Gal.5:19)

Climate Alarmism - breaks God's command.

Believing that people can control nature is one of the greatest stupidities in the history of the world. No human has ever been able to hold back a tsunami, stop a tornado or quench a volcano. To believe humans have God-like power to control nature is pure self-worship and the height of idolatrous pride.

You must not make an idol and bow down to it. For I am the LORD your God. (Lev.26:1)

The tip of the iceberg!

The well-constructed totalitarian agenda of the UN | UNESCO | WHO | WEF, and the small group of kings and wealthy 'elites' they serve, is the agenda of the Great Whore, whose purpose is to unite the world against the Laws of God and the Testimony of Christ. Her role is to gather the nations together and lead them into a final battle against God's people in the hope of wiping us off the face of the planet.

Babylon falls!

The Bible calls that final battle the Battle of Armageddon, a battle the Whore can't win. She is so blinded by her own pride she can't see that she is leading herself to her own doom.

> *Fallen, fallen is Babylon the Great! She has become a lair for demons and a haunt for every unclean spirit. (Rev.17:10)*

> *All the nations have drunk the wine of the passion of her immorality. The kings of the earth were immoral with her, and the merchants of the earth have grown wealthy from the extravagance of her luxury. (Rev.18:3)*

Just before the final battle begins, Christ returns, and we find it is the Great Whore, the two beasts and Satan himself, who end up being wiped off the face of the planet. The politics of the Earth vanish, and the politics of the Kingdom of God and Christ are established forever.

Coming out
from the Great Whore
is an action.

That is
the action of faith
Christ will be looking for
when he returns.

LIES HAVE BEEN COVERING THE TRUTH

CHAPTER 14

Revelation truths
are not meant
to be dark and scary.
They are meant
to reveal
the glory of Christ!

SHINING THE LIGHT

Are we at Armageddon yet? No! We are not surrounded yet. The nations are not united against Christianity yet. This is not the end. It's just evil in action. The only way to stop the spread of evil is to take counter-action. Our generation has the responsibility of tearing down this current evil.

Confusing the meaning of 'faith' is a key element in the enemy's deception. For, while they are busy taking action, they are telling God's people we don't need to take action, that personal 'faith' is all we need.

We overcome by the word of our testimony, and all the testimonies of Scripture result from visible actions of faith. *Without faith, it is impossible to please God. (Heb.11:6)* Satan's servants have used the very word that has the power to bring their plans undone (faith) as an opiate to keep us quiet.

It's time to shake off their lies and false perceptions and get back to the truth. Christians are not supposed to huddle in the dark while evil spreads unchecked across the world.

We carry the light!

No one will see the glorious light we carry if we don't let the light shine. We make up one-third of the world's population. No wonder the Great Whore wants to muzzle us and keep us quiet. We have the power to thwart her plans for total world domination.

How did I discover this?

For me, the Book of Revelation is a comforting light shining in the darkness. It is the most encouraging book I have ever read. It reveals the truth about Christ and brings Satan into proper focus. It holds the greatest hope the world has ever known and gives those going through the harshness of persecution quiet confidence as they await their final salvation.

It wasn't always that way. I didn't set out to understand the images of Revelation. Like many others, I'd heard so many contradictory theories that I'd put them all into the 'too hard basket' and decided not to worry about any of them. I didn't see Revelation as relevant to my normal Christian walk.

Until God changed my mind!

The perspective I now have of the revealed glory and absolute authority of Christ was given to me by God as an answer to a prayer for something else.

I had become so distressed by the ugliness of Satan's blasphemy raging against Christ in so many unexpected ways that I asked God to show me how to counteract its effect. God answered that prayer through the Book of Revelation.

This is what happened!

It was a quiet Sunday afternoon in 1981, and I had a few minutes to spare before leaving for church, so I flicked casually through the local newspaper.

When I turned to the entertainment guide, I saw an advertisement for a movie at the local club, and the name of the star caught my eye. It was 'Emmanuelle'.

It took me a few seconds to realise the movie being advertised was pornographic, and then I was horrified, not because pornography exists, but because the name this porn queen chose was the name of Christ.

I closed the paper and began to pray, talking to the Lord about the horror of the blasphemy I had just seen and then put it out of my mind and busied myself with other things.

That evening, during worship, the congregation began to sing *'Emanuel, God with us'*, and as I sang the name of Christ, I remembered the horrible advertisement and became angry that Satan's ugly blasphemy was intruding on my worship.

At that point, all I wanted to do was compensate my loving Saviour, somehow, for the injustice and hatred of the blatant blasphemy raging against him. I threw myself into prayer, and as I tried to lift up the name of Christ, I realised I didn't know how to lift his name in a way that would counter Satan's hatred.

So, I changed my prayer and asked God to teach me how to fight Satan's blasphemy. I didn't receive an answer straight away, and nothing came to mind that could help me understand how to pray.

I was filled with grief!

Intense sadness enveloped me like a heavy blanket, and for several days, I couldn't think about anything but the assault on the name of Christ. I felt small and useless in the face of what I was thinking and feeling because I didn't know what to do about it, so I continued to pray for understanding.

Then, the answer came!

Towards the end of the third day, I had a vague recollection that somewhere in the Book of Revelation there was something written about Satan's blasphemy of the name of Christ.

I picked up the Bible and turned to the Book of Revelation. The page that opened was Chapter 13, the one that talks about the beast with seven heads filled with blasphemous names, and what I saw at that moment left me stunned!

It was so simple!

The problem and its detailed solution were written right there in front of my eyes. All I had to do was read what was already written. The chapter started with 'and', so I followed the line of thought backwards and read the few verses before to find where the 'and' came from. There was the answer!

Within a few minutes, I learned that Satan's warfare is entirely directed at breaking down the Commandments of God and bringing blasphemy to the name and work of Christ, but also that God and Christ had put unassailable limits on his aggression.

I could suddenly see that God was totally in control! He allowed us to see Satan conjure this beast, for this beast showed us that the voluntary death of his Son had eternally flowing ramifications that Satan could not even begin to fight. This image clearly revealed that those who simply accept the victory of Christ's death and resurrection automatically share in his triumph over Satan.

Now I knew how to tear down the blasphemy of Satan. It wasn't complicated. It was just a matter of understanding the amazing power of the Gospel.

They overcame him by the Blood of the Lamb and the word of their testimony, and they loved not their lives so much as to shrink from death. (Rev.12:11)

I fell in love with Christ!

I began to read the Book of Revelation with new eyes, and as I did, I began to see the enormous depths of the love of God and Christ and the smallness of Satan in comparison.

Many years have passed since then, and throughout those years, I have never stopped learning. When God answers prayer, he is thorough.

I am now confident that I can share with others how to tear down the blasphemy of Satan running rampant across the world. More importantly, I know how to encourage believers to lift up the name of Christ in a way that will tear down blasphemy.

There is nothing more thrilling to me than to share what I know about the glorious might of our conquering Hero and the impervious Salvation he has so generously offered his beloved redeemed.

Old Law v New Law!

I also used to believe that the Old Testament Commandments were abolished by Christ and no longer needed to be considered, but that's not what this image in Revelation showed.

So, again, I asked God to teach me about the difference between the Old and New Commandments, and I would like to share what he taught me because God made it really clear that Mosiac Law is still relevant and will remain relevant to the end of days.

This is what he showed me!

In every Bible, when the New Commandment of Christ to *love God and love your neighbour as yourself* is written, it is cross-referenced to the original command of God in the Old Testament.

> *Do not seek revenge or bear a grudge against anyone among your people, but love your neighbour as yourself.*
> *(Lev.19:18)*

When Jesus chose this small verse of the Old Mosaic Law to be used as the second of his two New Commandments, he explained the reason for his choice to his disciples.

*'Love the Lord your God with all your
heart and with all your soul and with all
your mind.' This is the first and greatest
Commandment. And the second is like it:
'Love your neighbour as yourself.' All the
Law and the Prophets depend on these
two Commandments.* (Matt.22:37-40)

Jesus taught that *all the law and the Prophets
depend on these two Commandments.* It's easy
to see why we should love God with *all our heart,
mind, soul and strength,* but how does *not holding a
grudge* uphold all the law? How does *not holding a
grudge* equate to loving our neighbour the way God
wants our neighbour loved, and how does it help us
love our neighbour?

Part of the answer is found in the word 'grudge'
itself, for this is the same term used by God to
describe the grumbling and murmuring of his
people when they complained about Moses while
they were wandering in the desert of Sinai.

What those many Old Testament accounts
reveal is that those who held a grudge against
Moses were, in fact, holding a grudge against God
for making Moses their leader. We also learn that
God punished those who held a grudge by not
allowing them to enter the Promised Land.

This teaches us that when we hold a grudge
against anyone, we are, in reality, holding a grudge
against God for allowing them to affect our life.

So even when we know that what is being done is evil, our response must always be to *not hold a grudge*. For if we do, like the people of Israel, we will find ourselves on the wrong side of God's judgment.

Forgiveness is pivotal!

This is why forgiveness is so important and why we are told so emphatically to forgive. Only forgiveness destroys the power of a grudge and helps us to genuinely *love our neighbours*, including those who are our enemies, with Kingdom love.

Kingdom love is not worldly love. Kingdom love is shown in keeping the Commandments of God and encouraging others to keep them. This is the love that Christ is referring to when he speaks of *loving our neighbour as ourselves*.

> *This is how we love our neighbour, by loving God and keeping his Commandments. This is how we know we love God, by keeping his Commandments.* (1Jn.5:2-3)

When Christ gave us this New Law, he took us straight to the core of sin itself. He showed us that *holding a grudge* is behind the breaking of every Commandment, for without grumbling, murmuring or holding a grudge, no Law would ever be broken.

Forgiveness gets rid of every grudge and allows us to love our neighbour, our enemies, our families and everyone else in the purity of Kingdom love.

How does it work?

The first Commandment we break when we hold a grudge is the Commandment to love God with all our heart, for if we can't trust God with all the details of our lives, he doesn't have our hearts. The others are just as easy to see:

- If we don't hold a grudge against our spouse, we won't consider looking for a replacement spouse and, therefore, won't commit adultery.

- If we don't hold a grudge against the prosperous, including our employers, we won't covet their goods or consider stealing their possessions.

- If we don't hold a grudge against those who offend us and treat us badly, we won't take revenge or be tempted to kill.

- If we don't hold a grudge against the various people in our lives, we will not want to gossip about them, slander them, lie or promote any kind of false testimony about them.

- If we don't hold a grudge against our parents, whether we consider them to be perfect or not, we won't be tempted to dishonour them.

This is why *all the law and prophets* rest on these two Commandments of Christ, for if we learn the power of turning the temptation to grumble, murmur or hold a grudge into an opportunity for forgiveness, we fulfil both commands to *love God* and *love our neighbour* at the same time.

Loving our neighbour has nothing to do with feelings, emotions or socialism. Kingdom love upholds God's Commandments.

This is how we truly love our society, our nation, and our world; by bringing the love of Christ to them via the upholding of God's Commandments.

Action is still needed!

Not holding a grudge does not at all mean that we cease to take action against evil. On the contrary, when we forgive the people bringing the sin, it doesn't mean that we should allow the sin to continue doing harm. We still have the responsibility to confront it, resist it, condemn it and tear it down.

- Jesus didn't hold a grudge against anyone, but he still made a whip and cleansed the temple of the money changers. (Jn.2:14-16)

- Paul didn't hold a grudge against BarJesus, but he still pronounced blindness on him and had him led away from the Proconsul whom he was trying to deceive. (Acts 13:6-12)

- Peter didn't hold a grudge against Ananias and Sapphira, but he still pronounced the judgment of the Spirit on them, which brought their immediate deaths. (Acts 5:1-11)

We overcome not just by the *Blood of the Lamb* that covers others' sins as we forgive them, but by the *Word of our Testimony,* which exalts Christ and holds the power to tear down all blasphemy.

Two witnesses!

These three examples from Jesus, Paul and Peter show exactly what tearing down blasphemy looks like. God was being dishonoured *(Jesus)*, his Gospel was being trashed *(Paul)*, and his people were being deceived *(Peter)*. In each case, the Spirit of God powerfully upheld the First Commandment. Are these kinds of deeds still relevant today? Yes, they are!

In Revelation, there are two anointed witnesses described as *two olive branches* and *two lampstands*. John taught his disciples that the two anointed witnesses standing beside God are the *Word* and the *Spirit* (1 Jn. 5:7 KJV) (See also Zec.4:6-14). In other words, those who live by the Spirit and uphold God's Word will bear witness to the Spirit's authority to tear down blasphemy in four spoken ways:

- calling down fire from Heaven,
- holding back rain,
- turning rivers to blood, and
- pronouncing plagues at will.

That is exactly what the Old Testament prophets, like Moses and Elijah, were authorised to do. It's what Peter, Paul and all the disciples of Christ were authorised to do. Christ's disciples include you and me.

These witnesses have power to shut the sky so that no rain will fall...and power to turn the waters into blood and to strike the earth with every kind of plague as often as they wish. (Rev.11:6)

Enormous authority!

When rulers and others rise up *against* God, God's people need to rise up *for* God. But to do so, like the disciples, we first need to make a definite choice. Will we serve God or man?

In the Book of Acts, we read the account of Peter and John, who had just been called before the Sanhedrin and forbidden to preach the Gospel.

> *But Peter and John replied, "Judge for yourselves whether it is right in God's sight to listen to you rather than God. (Acts 4:19)*

When they were released, again with orders not to preach the Gospel under threat of arrest, the other believers gathered to hear what had happened, and their immediate response was this prayer.

> *Why do the nations rage and the peoples plot in vain? The kings of the earth take their stand and the rulers gather together against the Lord and against His Anointed One. (Acts 4:26-27)*

> *Now, Lord, consider their threats, and enable your servants to speak your word with complete boldness, while you stretch out your hand to heal and perform signs and wonders through the name of your holy servant Jesus. (Acts 4:29-30)*

The perfect prayer for this present darkness!

Turn on the light!

Peter and John understood the power of their Kingdom authority. They understood the necessity of *gathering together* with other believers and being *faithful in prayer*. But they also understood that *going into the world* to boldly spread the message of the Kingdom was the key to experiencing miracles. It was the only way for people in the world to witness first-hand the authority and power of the Gospel.

False prophets in the churches have convinced believers to disobey Christ's Great Commission, telling us prayer and gathering with other believers is enough. It isn't! Or the day of miracles has passed. It hasn't! Or that we need credentials before we go. We don't! Obeying Christ's Commission is the only way to shine the light of Christ into this dark world.

'Going' is where miracles live!

Biblical history shows that miracles happen when God's people do more than gather for worship and prayer! It also shows that so many mighty miracles resulted from taking a stand against political oppression, it could be concluded that Faith + Politics = Miracles. Here are a few more examples:

- Daniel in the Lion's Den (Political)
- Shadrach, Meshach and Abednego (Political)
- Joshua and the Fall of Jerico (Political)
- Gideon and the Midianites (Political)
- Elisha blinding the Syrian army (Political)

Imagine what it would be like today if billions of God's redeemed suddenly decided to venture out of their churches and embrace the Great Commission. God would work with us to unleash his mighty love, salvation, justice, healing, comfort and deliverance over the world *as the waters cover the sea (Hab.2:14)*. Would this put a dint in the current political aggression? It certainly would!

I tell you the truth, anyone who believes in me will do the works I have been doing, and they will do even greater works, because I am going to the Father.

You can ask anything in my name, and I will do it, so that the Son can bring glory to the Father. (John 14:12-13)

Faith in action *will* overcome the world!

The works Christ is talking about above and commands us to do through his Great Commission are actions of faith. They are works that involve miracles, signs and wonders. The world is filled with pain, suffering, heartbreak, lies, confusion, sickness, and fear. Do we have the authority and power to overcome this present darkness? Yes! We do!

Everyone who is born of God overcomes the world. And this is the victory that overcomes the world; our faith. (1John 5:4)

The light we shine is 'works'!

Let your light
so shine before men,
that they may
see your good works
and glorify your Father
who is in Heaven

- Matt.5:16 -

WE CAN STOP THE DEVASTATION

CHAPTER 15

Can our actions
stop
the establishment
of the
New World Order?
Yes!

IT'S BEEN DONE BEFORE

Does good overcome evil? Yes! All the evil in this world comes through people. The 'antichrist spirit' in people is all around us, all the time. Currently, it is being forced on billions by a few wealthy elites and their boot-lickers. But good also comes through people. And the good of many can overcome the evil of the few. We've seen it happen many times!

Today, good, peace-loving people are being trained not to oppose, resist, or fight the evil New World Order. We are being dumbed down, not just with false doctrine in the churches but in the world as well, with everyone being driven to go along with the herd - or else!

The media and politicians are polluting our minds with inane 'left' v 'right' concepts and constant political infighting to prevent us from asking the right questions about where this evil is taking the world.

Where are they taking us?

It's easier to see the overarching plans of the proposed New World Order when we investigate its origins and see what makes its advocates tick.

When we look at the foundational truths on which the elites have based their ruthless agenda, it becomes obvious their New World Order concept is doomed to failure. It's been done before, several times! It has failed before, several times! In the following pages, you will see what they are emulating and why it will fail again.

THE 'NEW WORLD ORDER' IS NOT SO NEW!

The origin of the United Nations logo is very telling. It incorporates the logo of the Roman Republic (509BC-47BC), which ended with the violent assassination of Julius Caesar.

SPQR: The Senate and the People of Rome.

OLIVE WREATH: Did not symbolise peace. It crowned the heads of the brutal elite rulers and symbolised their absolute power.

It doesn't take a genius to see that one emblem resembles the other. The big question is, why would the United Nations choose an emblem with such strong connections to the Old World Order of an obsolete dictatorship? Is it because the Roman Republic is not obsolete but simply functioning in another form? It appears so! Let's take a look...

THE OLD WORLD ORDER

THE NEW WORLD ORDER

212

THE OLD WORLD ORDER

The land conquered by the Roman Republic, later known as the Roman Empire, covered the area on the logo map from Britain across Europe to the Holy Land. It was a totalitarian republic.

Prior to the Roman Republic, Rome was a monarchy, but in 509BC the wealthy families seized control. Fifty oligarchs created a power cooperative, which they called a Senate. From there, they controlled the appointment of magistrates, military officers and priests, using their absolute power to increase their landholdings and oppress the rest of society.

Observation: In 1945, fifty nations created a power cooperative and called it the United Nations. Their aim was to ensure 'peace' through the absolute control of International Law, International Military and Policing, and International Religious Practice.

The ordinary Roman workers and business people, called *'plebeians'*, had only one option open to them to fight the greedy and brutal oppression of the wealthy Senators, *'secessio plebis'*, the cessation of labour and services to the wealthy. This is what we call 'strike action', and it worked! Through their strikes, the people gained the protection of both civil and religious laws and the right to vote. That vote was called a *'plebiscite'*.

Once they could vote, the people placed plebeian representatives inside the Senate with the power to veto unwelcome Senate decisions and block elections of new Senators. These representatives were called 'tribunes'.

Observation: This was the beginning of the 'two-house' system of government. To this day, political infighting between 'left and right' houses is still supposed to represent the struggle between the goals of the rich and the good of the people. But that falls apart if both sides are wealthy.

The election of tribunes led to decades of political infighting until the tribunes finally succumbed to the will of the oligarchs. United, they became the 'elites', and their new goal was the increase of landholdings and personal wealth via the conquest of surrounding nations. Wars became normal. As each nation fell, the elites selected and installed 'puppet-leaders' from within each fallen nation who would, for financial reward, willingly serve the Republic rather than their own people.

Observation: As the United Nations puts more and more pressure on nations to accept their international laws and totalitarian controls, they install and reward 'puppet-leaders' who willingly serve them rather than their own people.

The wealth and power of the ruling elites of the Senate of Rome grew, but so did corruption and self-interest, and it wasn't long before laws were made for the interests of the few ruling elites rather than for the good of the people of the broadening Republic.

Observation: Government corruption and the self-interest of leaders within the governments of the Western world have grown like cancers since the inception of the United Nations, and laws are now made to indemnify the actions of corrupt politicians.

Moral decay, chaos, instability, famine, slavery and the rise of widespread social unrest became the new normal in the Roman Republic until the people said 'enough' and active plans to overthrow the corrupt government system led to civil war.

Observation: Moral decay, chaos, instability, food shortages and poverty, which all lead to slavery, are being used like weapons to destroy the stability and freedom of peaceful democracies. This will only stop when the people say 'enough'!

After a century of social unrest, insurrections and civil war, the Roman Republic collapsed and in 27BC was replaced by the Roman Empire. It was basically a return to the monarchical system, albeit with an elected Emperor instead of a King.

AN UNDERGROUND EMPIRE

The Roman Empire came to an inglorious end in 1453AD but did not disappear into oblivion. It simply went underground and took on a hidden form. Its ambition to rule the world continued through its network of 'puppet-nations'. In this way, it became unaccountable for any atrocities committed by those nations, and as it now had no national lands that could be taken in reprisal, it became 'untouchable'.

Observation: The United Nations uses 'puppet-nations' to do its bidding. It is not accountable for their actions and has no lands that can be conquered. It leaches off the wealth of the nations, and without that wealth, it would die. This means it can be stopped!

The 'hidden' Roman Empire was ruled by a succession of elected leaders bestowed with titles only given to Emperors of Rome. A well-known alternate title to Emperor was Caesar, but a not-so-well-known title was 'Pontifex Maximus' chief high priest of religion or Pontiff. Yes, the Pope is the elected Emperor of Rome. He can't hold the tile of Pontifex Maximus without holding the other Imperial titles as well.

Observation: *Despite popular belief, the Apostle Peter was not the first Pope. He was never an Emperor of Rome and so could not hold that title.*

In the role of Emperor of Rome, various Popes ordered nations to invade other nations and install Catholicism as the national religion. Wealthy Bishops and Cardinals were planted to ensure 'puppet-monarchs' would continue to serve Rome.

So-called 'holy' wars were fought continually for centuries. The most notable were the Crusader wars in the Holy Land as Rome sought to regain possession of Jerusalem, previously conquered under the Roman Republic and still ruled during the time of Christ. It was the Roman Empire, under the second Emperor/ Pontiff(Pope) *Tiberius Caesar,* that put Christ to death.

Over time, Britain, France and Spain all tried to *'rule the waves'* in the name of Rome. They were pitted against each other as they sailed to distant shores with the hope of being the first to discover and claim uncharted lands. They went with the Pope's 'blessing', supposedly for the glory of their nation, but in reality, to spread Rome's influence through Catholicism.

THE RISE OF THE NEW WORLD ORDER

The last nation conquered by *Julius Caesar* before the collapse of the Roman Republic was Britain. Britain had no written history before its acquiescence to Rome, and its first recorded king, *Mandubracius*, was a 'puppet-monarch' installed by *Julius Caesar* to serve the interests of the Republic.

Britain started as a Roman 'puppet-monarchy', and over hundreds of years, various Popes ordered incursions to ensure Britain would remain a servant of the Roman Empire. Politically loyal Bishops and Cardinals compelled British monarchs to serve Rome until Henry VIII broke away from Catholicism and founded the Anglican Church.

But the damage was done!

As the population increased, and while Rome was still directly involved, a fledgling parliament was established to 'assist' the monarch to rule. With the advice and help of loyal Papists, it reflected the government style of the Roman Republic, including a Senate, House of Lords, House of Commons and a vote for the common man. So, despite the later removal of direct Papal influence, Roman authority was firmly embedded.

Observation: *Today, it's easy to see why the establishment of the United Nations, its logo and various charters were largely influenced by notable Britons. Britain enthusiastically embraced the Roman Republic's style of government, including the long-standing Roman goal of world domination.*

RUTHLESS | INVISIBLE | UNACCOUNTABLE

Adopting the symbol of the iron-fisted rule of the original despotic Roman elites shows the intention of the United Nations to gain wealth and power for today's globalists via the conquest of nations and the installation of national 'puppet-leaders' who serve the United Nations rather than their own people.

Adopting the same 'Modus Operandi' as the hidden Roman Empire further shows the intention of the United Nations to wield absolute power through servile 'puppet-nations' who bear the brunt of any reprisals while the UN remains 'untouchable'.

In the same way that the Pope falsely presents himself to the world as a beacon of 'purity and holiness', so the United Nations falsely presents itself to the world as a beacon of 'care and protection'. But the truth is an entirely different story.

The invisible Roman Empire continues to pursue its role of world domination. And, though that reality remains hidden under a thick religious veil, centuries of actions reveal the truth.

Likewise, though the United Nations presents an innocent facade, their charters and organisations clearly reveal they want complete global control over law, government, the military, policing, health, education, food, media, religion, land, minerals, banking and every person on the planet. It's no wonder their logo shows the world inside a target.

They want it all!

BLATANT MANIPULATION AND CONTROL

The greatest threat to the United Nations' New World Order is the Christian-based ideology of the general population. We believe in and uphold freedom, equality, justice, the value of human life, morality, peace, love, hope and much more - values that the Roman Republic detested and feared and the Roman Empire controlled and exploited.

The United Nations and all its organisations pretend to uphold the values listed above, but they don't. They actually endorse and promote the opposite of all those values. The easiest way to see what they really believe is to take a look at their attitudes to climate change. What they say and what they endorse are two different things!

A tried and true method!

The Roman Empire, under Constantine, altered doctrine to take control of Christianity and corral Christians within a state-run religion, Catholicism. It exploited those who truly love God and Christ by using them to gain wealth and spread Rome's power and influence throughout the known world.

Emulating their methods, the United Nations is also using altered doctrine to take control of Christians, but that's not all. It is using altered climate data to take control of environmentalists. It exploits those who love nature and truly care for the planet by using them to grow the global wealth, power and influence of its oligarch masters.

While innocent children are taught to believe that 'green energy' and 'net zero' are the responsible way forward, it's not true. The real cost of solar panels, wind turbines and 'eco-friendly' electric vehicles is total environmental destruction.

Mining for the rare earth minerals needed to create batteries to capture the energy gained from wind and solar and to drive eco-*un*friendly vehicles is the most toxic mining on the planet.

Delivering 'net zero' green energy targets will not only cause widespread destruction of the planet into the future, it is already costing the lives of people, animals, fish and birds and killing vegetation that comes into contact with the deadly, carcinogenic toxins released into the land and water in the mined areas.

Green Greed Energy!

Green Energy should be called Greed Energy. The only people who benefit are the greedy masterminds of the 'climate change' myth, whose green energy products rape the world and do unfixable environmental harm. Here are just a few reports.

DEVASTATION IN CHINA

China began mining for rare earth minerals in 1990 and set up chemical processing factories to refine those minerals. The resultant cancer epidemics and data on air, water and soil pollution were treated as 'state secrets' until 2013, when it was estimated there were around 450 cancer villages in China, with that number growing.

Later in 2013, a separate government survey reported that 16.1% of China's soil and 19.4% of farmland were contaminated, affecting villagers, reducing harvests and rendering much of China's homegrown food toxic.

(China's Dirty Secret: The Boom Poisoned Its Soil and Crops. Written by He Guangwei, Yale School of the Environment, 30 June, 2014)

In 2017, the Chinese government shut down rare earth mineral mining in China.

Mining for rare earth minerals generates large volumes of toxic and radioactive material due to the co-extraction of thorium and uranium— radioactive metals which can cause problems for the environment and human health. (Reported by Australia's CSIRO to Misha Ketchell, Editor, The Conversation, 16 April, 2021)

MYANMAR IS DESTROYED

One of China's neighbours, Myanmar, is now China's single largest source of rare earth minerals, making up 70% of global supply, according to *Chinese Customs* data and *United Nations* trade data. But at what cost?

More than 2700 leaching pools dot what used to be fertile farmlands and pristine forests. The river water is no longer drinkable, endangered species such as tigers, pangolins, and red pandas have fled, and fish have become extinct. The various acids used in extraction are so strong they eat through the shovels of bulldozers and excavators.

Armed militia force farmers off their land unless they 'choose' to profit from rare earth mineral mining, threatening them and their children with death by shooting. However, even when they comply, the locals are left with nothing. *"They are mining rare earth minerals everywhere, and we are no longer safe to drink water,"* said one brave villager. *"There is nothing to support the children. Nothing to eat."*

(The Sacrifice Zone: Myanmar bears cost of green energy. Published by Dake Kang, Victoria Milko and Lori Hinnant in AP News, 10 August, 2022)

This is the real cost of 'green energy'

It doesn't take long to deplete a country of its rare earth mineral supplies, which are not found in 'veins' as are gold or coal but are scattered through the topsoils of open spaces like farmlands. And, as 250 tons of topsoil needs to be mined to gain enough minerals for ONE electric car battery, filling the world with electric cars can only be described as irresponsibly destructive.

Rare earth minerals are not renewable, and once they are gone, they are gone for good. What they leave behind is a toxic wasteland. The United Nations knows all this but does nothing to stop the devastation.

Where is the United Nations?

- Has the UN come to the aid of the poor, displaced people of Myanmar whose once fertile lands are now so toxic they are no longer habitable? No!

- Has the UN come to the aid of the people living in the 450 designated 'cancer towns' of China? No!

- Has the UN come to the aid of the 40,000 children of the African Congo being used to mine cobalt? No!

- Has the UN mentioned the need to protect vital food-producing farmlands from the toxic outcomes of rare earth mineral mining? No!

None of the above would be happening **at all** if the United Nations were not actively promoting the climate change myth for the fiscal benefit of the elites. All this pain is their doing! They are not going to stop it! They are the catalyst!

This toxic mess is not the outworking of duplicity, accident or oversight. This is the true face of the United Nations. These facts show who they really are and will always be. What the 'untouchable' United Nations has planned for the world under their proposed New World Order is exceedingly dark and dangerous but not inevitable.

People have power!

The great lesson we learn from looking back at the Old World Order is that tyrannical elites depend on the general population to meet their needs. If ordinary people wake up to their schemes and revolt, the despots lose their power. The good thing is that the general population of the Western world is made up of kind and caring people, the overwhelming majority of whom are Christians. We can stop this!

THE TRUTH WILL ALWAYS SET US FREE!

I have shown you this highly condensed overview of 2,500 years of the world's political history so that you can see its direct effect on the global events currently manipulating the Western world.

What the world is going through now is not new. The Old Roman World Order has been meticulously updated with technological controls and communist coercion tactics and relaunched under a new name.

The goals of the oligarchs and elite merchants behind this New World Order are not new either. They are still identical to the goals of the Great Whore described in Scripture so long ago. They still want to rule the world; they still want to bribe and coerce kings and national leaders to subjugate their people and use them to gain more wealth and power; and they are still prepared to break every moral and natural law in order to achieve their goals.

It's an old story!

The two beasts and Great Whore described for us by Christ in the Book of Revelation were familiar to the people of John's day. They recognised the Great Whore because they were also living under the influence and control of the Roman Empire.

The most amazing thing about the true message of Revelation is that, in it, Christ teaches us how to overcome the two beasts and the Great Whore. Is that not the most important message in the world today? That is exactly what the world needs to hear!

We can overcome!

Is it any wonder the true message of Revelation has been targetted, altered, re-written and presented to Christians in a way that will blind us to the power we have to overcome this current evil.

I have said these things to you, that in me you may have peace. In the world you will have tribulation. But take heart; I have overcome the world. (John 16:33)

While he was on earth, Christ lived under the confines of Roman rule. He taught his disciples how to overcome even while they were living under Roman rule. What he taught back then is exactly what we need to hear today. We need to learn from Christ how to overcome as he overcame.

Christ's blueprint for success!

The Roman Empire, even at the peak of its power, could not stop Christianity from growing and spreading the Good News of Christ's Great Commission. It could not overcome the message of the Gospel.

Revelation teaches that even at the end of time, when all the political forces of the nations unite and gather around us, they still can't overcome us. Christ's Gospel is unstoppable!

The darkness in the world today will not overcome Christians. We carry the light! The Gospel is the light, and Christ's Great Commission is his blueprint for our success as we take his light to the world.

His way works!

The United Nations' New World Order is not sustainable long-term, and the elites know it. It is based on the Old World Order, which failed miserably several times. Do they care? No! They are so driven by greed that if they gained all the wealth of the world, it would still not be enough. Meanwhile, the damage and suffering they are currently causing is cruel, unnecessary and diabolic. It must stop!

We can stop it!

In the world, Christians need to start boldly standing up for God's law, informing others of the real cost of the UN | UNESCO | WHO | WEF agenda, and asking politicians and media personalities to explain what they are doing to address the hidden devastation.

In the churches, we need to expose the politically driven lying doctrines, myths and fantasies, walk away from those who teach them, and get back to the Gospel.

Go into all the world and preach the Gospel to every creature. Whoever believes and is baptised will be saved, but whoever does not believe will be condemned.

And these signs will accompany those who believe: In my name, they will drive out demons; they will speak in new tongues; they will pick up snakes with their hands, and if they drink any deadly poison, it will not harm them; they will lay their hands on the sick, and they will be made well. (Matt.28:15:18)

Does
the Gospel
have the power
to save the world?

Yes!

It's the only thing
that does!

TRAINED UP - FOR SUCH A TIME AS THIS

THE AUTHOR

Write the vision
make it plain,
so that he who
reads it,
will run with it.

- Hab.2:2 -

MONICA BENNETT-RYAN

Hi, I'm Monica!

Thank you for taking the time
to read this little book.

Who am I?

I'm an Australian who has actively served Christ since my early twenties. I'm a mother of three and grandmother of eight, and I believe I have been trained by God in the area covered by this book *for such a time as this (Esther 4:14)*. I firmly believe this is not the time for the redeemed to remain quiet.

I have not remained quiet. Between 2009 and 2012, I successfully stood as a whistleblower against corruption in Australia's Defence Intelligence, which was at that time putting Australia's National Security and our military at risk.

Exposing the corruption was not easy. Jail time was a real threat. In Australia, people who blow the whistle on government corruption or threaten government commercial interests can be jailed for between five and twenty years. So, I had a lot on the line when I stepped out in faith with two other Christians to take a stand for righteousness.

We took a huge risk by going public without any physical proof. The evidence was digital, locked inside highly secure Defence computers and inaccessible to anyone outside Defence Intelligence. Yet, despite this major hurdle plus many Defence threats, legal games and media tactics, we successfully exposed the corruption, took it to the highest court in Australia, stayed out of jail, and won! Then, after our victory, the three of us were vindicated in the media and honoured in Parliament for our efforts.

The parliament owes these three brave people a great debt of gratitude.
(Senator Johnston, Parliament, 9 Feb 2012)

When Covid and the lockdowns hit, I recognised the same patterns of coercion and corruption I had stood against in my battle with Defence, and so, I am currently doing all I can to assist those who are standing against the clouds of evil rolling across the world through the UN | UNESCO | WHO | WEF alliance.

I would encourage all Christians to make their voice heard on social issues. If Christians don't actively stand for righteousness in society, who will?

I have written several books including a sequal to *The Antichrist Deception.* Titled *The Apostate Church,* it exposes various other entrenched political doctrines masquerading as truth, explains why Christian leadership remains quiet while evil forces tear down morality and Christian values, and shows from Scripture what we can do.

I have listed a few of my books in the following pages, including a series of ebooks that I give away free on Kindle Unlimited. The ebook versions of my print books are also free on Kindle Unlimited. This ebook will remain free as long as Amazon allows.

Please help me spread this message by leaving a one or two word comment on Amazon. Every little bit helps to shine the light. Thank you.

Be blessed!

NATIONAL
SECURITY
FOR SALE

We knew the truth could cost us our freedom!

This true story takes you behind the scenes of Australia's Defence Intelligence, reveals secrets, and uncovers government corruption that crosses Party boundaries and goes all the way to the top.

It is the only eye-witness account of the entrenched and systemic government disinformation that put ASIO and our National Security at risk. Are they still at risk? You decide!

"This book is about the selling of our Intelligence Agencies. National Security should never be outsourced!"
Senator Gerard Rennick, 2025.

IN HIS NAME
PUBLISHING

www.inhisname.com.au

An Eye-Opening

TRUE STORY

MONICA BENNETT-RYAN

NATIONAL SECURITY FOR SALE

THE DARK SIDE OF AUSTRALIA'S DEFENCE INTELLIGENCE

TOP SECRET

NATIONAL SECURITY FOR SALE MONICA BENNETT-RYAN

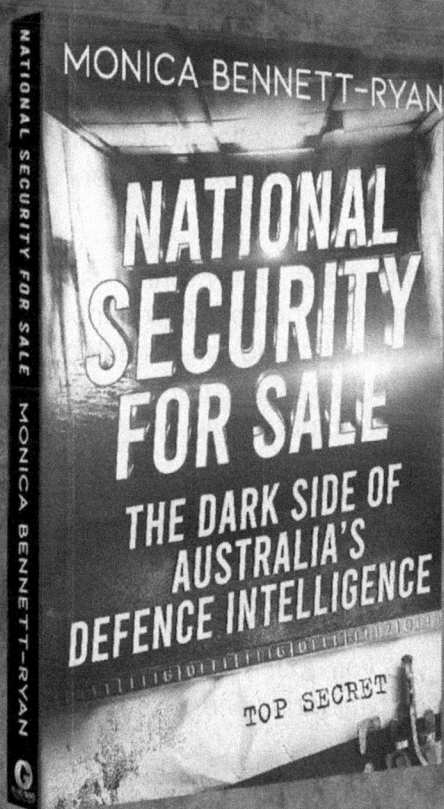

Of Government Enforced
Misinformation & Disinformation

THE APOSTATE
CHURCH

Heaven is the reward for those who fulfil the terms of the New Covenant.

This book questions whether Christianity is based on devotion to Christ or to a denomination. Two very different things!

Being part of the New Covenant priesthood set up by Christ is different from being a member of a denomination and submitting to credentialed clergy. Those activities are not part of Christ's New Covenant contract.

The assumption that we can abandon Christ's New Covenant priesthood model, follow paid clergy instead, and still gain eternal life is just not true!

Will you go to Heaven? Have you fulfilled the terms of the New Covenant?

IN HIS NAME
PUBLISHING

www.inhisname.com.au

HORRIFYING

**THE GREATEST DECEPTION
SINCE ADAM AND EVE
TOOK SATAN'S BAIT**

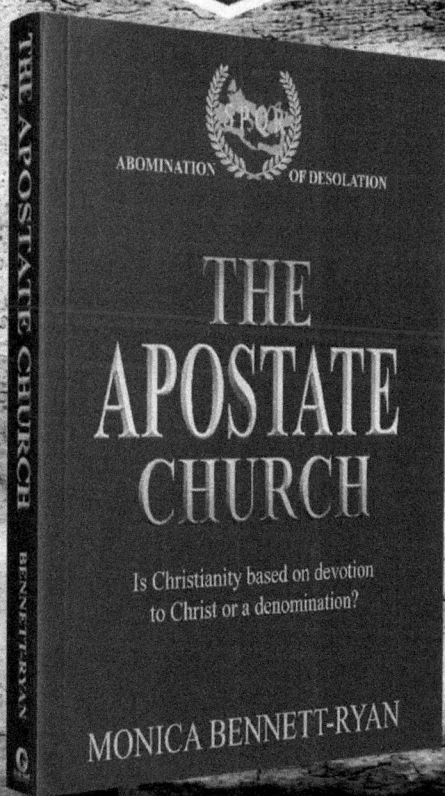

ABOMINATION OF DESOLATION

THE APOSTATE CHURCH

Is Christianity based on devotion
to Christ or a denomination?

MONICA BENNETT-RYAN

THE APOSTATE CHURCH

BENNETT-RYAN

REVELATION
ANCIENT AND MYSTERIOUS

Blessed are those who read and understand what is written. (Rev.1:3)

Revelation is not scary or frightening!

All the symbols and images contained within that beautiful book bring us good news and tidings of great joy.

They are given to comfort and bless and remind us that no matter how how many obstacles Christ's enemies may lay before the redeemed, our triumphant Saviour has been there before us, shown us the way to victory and given us his power and authority to also overcome the world.

IN HIS NAME
PUBLISHING

www.inhisname.com.au

How did the ancient dynamic of Heaven change after Christ was raised from the dead?

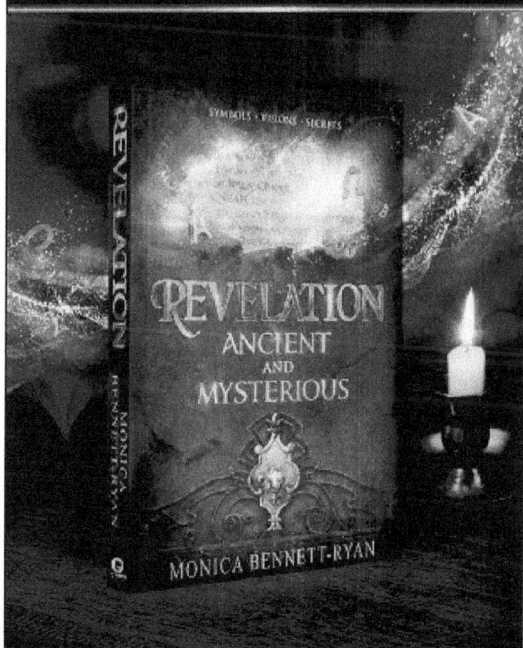

SYMBOLS · VISIONS · SECRETS

REVELATION
ANCIENT
AND
MYSTERIOUS

MONICA BENNETT-RYAN

What do Revelation's signs, symbols, codes and visions really reveal?

VIRTUAL
- TO -
REALITY

In a time of chaos, when the world seems to have gone mad, comes a story of hope.

Though set in a fantasy world, the trials encountered and overcome in this book are current.

Deception, poisoning, lying, confusion, threats, division, betrayal, persecution, destruction of values and the looming threat of war.

Can a small group of ordinary teens overcome the dragon's two beastly pets and the vicious schemes of his wicked queen?

Enter the seven mighty Fire Lords...

IN HIS NAME
PUBLISHING

www.inhisname.com.au

FREE EBOOKS

LOVING God is love, and love was around before creation. *SO,* if love existed before any human emotions, feelings, sex or families, what is love?

JUDGING Jesus told us to forgive, and forgiveness is a judgment. *SO,* does that mean we can't forgive unless we first judge someone has done wrong?

HEAVEN Adam and Eve ate the fruit of 'good' and 'evil'. *SO,* does that mean 'good' is the same as 'evil'? Can being 'good' keep us out of heaven?

CURSING We're freed from all curses by the blood of Christ. *SO,* why was Paul tortured by a 'thorn in the flesh'? Wasn't that a curse?

TITHING Old Testament tithes paid for the forgiveness of sin. *SO,* since Jesus paid the price for our sins, should Christians tithe?

GOING Jesus commanded all his disciples to 'go' in his name. *SO,* do we need credentials first? What does it mean to go 'in his name'?

www.inhisname.com.au

The
EBOOK COLLECTION

LOVING
What a loaded word!

JUDGING
Should Christians Judge?

HEAVEN
What will it be like?

CURSING
Is it from God or Satan?

TITHING
Should Christians Tithe?

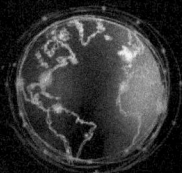

GOING
Did Jesus mean me?

SAY NO TO ENFORCED GLOBAL SLAVERY

MORE INFO

THEY PLAN TO DESTROY US

"You will own nothing and be happy."
- Klaus Schwab - CEO of WEF -

"Smart Cities will lock up humanity inside open-air concentration camps."
https://stopworldcontrol.com/smart-city/

THEY PLAN TO DESTROY OUR CHILDREN

Toddlers are encouraged to engage in "early childhood masturbation".

- WHO EDUCATIONAL MATERIAL -
https://stopworldcontrol.com/whosex

"Teach 5-year-olds to show love and care through sexual behaviours."

- DECLARED UN POLICY -
https://stopworldcontrol.com/children

THEY PLAN TO DESTROY OUR COUNTRY

"Globalists are determined to submit all of humanity to unprecedented tyranny through their Great Reset, Agenda21, Agenda 2030, and the New World Order".

- FIND OUT HOW TO STOP THEM -
https://stopworldcontrol.com/world-domination/

A FEW RESOURCES

Now that you see, you can begin to take action. Read books, educate yourself. Take notice of what is happening in politics. This planned destruction of lives doesn't have to happen. You can help stop it!

WHO IS 'STOP WORLD CONTROL.COM'?

Stop World Control is a Christian website set up by the founder of *Hope for Humanity* ministries, David Sorensen. David holds a master's degree in media and communication and works as a *'missionary journalist'* to report on critical truths that are censored by mainstream news media. He has a large, worldwide audience.

https://stopworldcontrol.com/about/

THE UNESCO CHARTER, published in 1946

In his charter, Julian Huxley calls for a single world government and goes on to discuss the importance of population control (i.e., mass murder).

https://archive.org/details/huxley-unesco-its-purpose-and-philosophy

** The information about the widespread influence of the Huxley family in setting forth the concepts of the UN and UNESCO was researched and first raised in an article by Robert W Malone MD, MS.**

https://rwmalonemd.substack.com/p/the-future-is-now

BRAVE NEW WORLD published in 1932

This book, written by Aldous Huxley, brother of the founder of UNESCO, Julian Huxley, is the stylised 'vision' of the Huxley's planned New World Order. Written before World War II, it includes the myth of overpopulation, the power of propaganda, use of chemicals for persuasion and the prohibition of monogamy, privacy, money and family. If you want to know why the UN was really set up, read this book.

https://www.amazon.com.au/Brave-New-World-Revisited/dp/0060776099

COVID-19: THE GREAT RESET

Klaus Schwab, CEO of the WEF, outlines how a new totalitarian one-world government will reduce all non-elites to slaves. The forced reset of our global social, economic, and political systems, which he says will result from Covid-19, will usher in a New World Order where people *'will own nothing and be happy".*

https://www.amazon.com.au/COVID-19-Great-Reset-Klaus-Schwab-ebook/dp/B08CRZ9VZB

THE REAL ANTHONY FAUCI

Robert Kennedy Jr. details how Fauci, Gates, and their cohorts control media outlets, scientific journals, key government agencies, intelligence agencies, scientists and physicians to flood the public with fearful propaganda, muzzle debate, and ruthlessly censor dissent.

https://www.amazon.com.au/Real-Anthony-Fauci-Democracy-Humanity/dp/1510766804

GREEN MURDER

Dr Ian Plimmer, a leading Australian geologist and Professor Emeritus at the University of Melbourne, says, "I charge the greens with murder! They murder humans who are kept in poverty without coal-fired electricity. They murder forests and wildlife by clear felling for rare earth minerals and wind turbines. They murder economies producing unemployment, hopelessness, the collapse of communities, social breakdown and suicide".

https://www.amazon.com.au/Green-Murder-Ian-Plimer/dp/1922449822

LIES MY GOVERNMENT TOLD ME

Dr Robert Malone, the inventor of the mRNA and DNA vaccination technologies, offers a comprehensive look at the Covid-19 pandemic. Challenging the government-pharma-media narrative, this book will not only outrage readers but also inform and give hope.

https://www.amazon.com.au/Lies-My-Govt-Told-Me/dp/151077324X

ONENESS VS THE 1%

Vandana Shiva explains how breaking free of the elite 1% and their constructs is not just possible; it has become necessary! She takes on the billionaires Gates and Zuckerberg and others whose greed has wrought havoc across the globe and proposes a safer, healthier way forward.

https://www.amazon.com/Oneness-vs-1-Shattering-Illusions/dp/1645020398

REVELATION: ANCIENT AND MYSTERIOUS

Peeling back Revelation's layers of symbolism, this book obliterates the introduced horror stories, reveals how Christ's powerful death culminated in an even more powerful resurrection and unveils the supreme authority bestowed on Christ because of Calvary.

Using simple terminology, the author takes the mystery out of the perplexing vision of the ten-horned beast, his mark and number, the second beast and the woman that accompanies them, explains the amazing roles of the seven Spirits, four living creatures, two witnesses and three demonic frogs, and brings to life the heart-pounding imagery of the four horsemen, seven seals, armageddon and the end of the world.

https://www.amazon.com.au/Revelation-Ancient-Mysterious-Monica-Bennett-Ryan/dp/0645351342

SPQR: A HISTORY OF ANCIENT ROME

SPQR is a definitive history of Ancient Rome. It explores democracy, migration, religious controversy, social mobility and exploitation and informs us that ancient Rome still matters. Its history of empire, conquest, cruelty and excess is something against which we still judge ourselves. Its myths and stories - from Romulus and Remus to the Rape of Lucretia - still strike a chord with us. And its debates about citizenship, security and the rights of the individual still influence our own debates on civil liberty today.

https://www.amazon.com.au/SPQR-History-Ancient-Mary-Beard/dp/184668381

CONSTANTINE VERSES CHRIST:
A Triumph of Ideology

Dr Alistair Kee argues that Constantine was not a Christian for, to Constantine, religion was part of an Imperial strategy. Using Christianity for his own ends, Constantine transformed it into something completely different. Along with his biographer and panegyrist Eusebius, he succeeded in replacing the norms of Christ and the early church with the norms of Imperial ideology.

Why it has been previously thought that Constantine was a Christian is not because what he believed was Christian, but because what he believed came to be called Christianity. Christianity became a 'triumph of ideology".

https://www.amazon.com.au/Constantine-Versus-Christ-Triumph-Ideology/dp/149829572X

FOLLOWING CHRIST

Charles Spurgeon encourages believers to step out and move into Christian action without waiting for credentials. He emphasises simply moving forward, using the talents and resources already at our disposal, for the Lord's service and our own eternal reward.

The concepts presented in this book are easy to understand. We must not simply take Christ as our Friend, but also as our Master. If we are to become His disciple, we must also become His servant. *His servants shall serve Him: and they shall see His face (Rev 22:3-4).*

https://www.amazon.com/Following-Christ-Annotated-Updated-Losing-ebook/dp/B07KTG2N2S

THE GLOBAL SEXUAL REVOLUTION:
Destruction of Freedom in the Name of Freedom

In her book, Gabriele Kuby surveys gender ideology and LGBT demands, the devastating effects of pornography and sex education, attacks on freedom of speech and religion, the corruption of language, and much more. It is a call to action for all well-meaning people to redouble their efforts to preserve freedom of religion, of speech, and of parents to educate their children so that the family may endure as the foundation upon which any healthy society is built.

https://www.amazon.com.au/Global-Sexual-Revolution-Gabriele-Kuby/dp/1621381544

THE CREATURE FROM JEKYLL ISLAND

Edward Griffin writes about the cause of wars, boom-bust cycles, inflation, depression, prosperity and bank bailouts that are nothing less than legalised plunder. He exposes the men behind the Federal Reserve and their inaugural meeting on Jekyll Island.

He takes an honest and logical look at the United Nations and how their New World Order's government system is designed to become the ultimate laboratory for social experiments upon mankind. He makes the point that the New World Order incubating in the United Nations cannot save the world from totalitarianism because it *is* totalitarianism.

https://www.amazon.com.au/Creature-Jekyll-Island-Federal-Reserve/dp/091298645X

GREEN TYRANNY

According to the author of the best-selling book *"Green Tyranny: Exposing the Totalitarian Roots of the Climate Industrial Complex"*, virtually every theme you see in the modern environmental movement was developed by the Nazis.

In his timely and provocative book, Rupert Darwall traces the alarming origins of the green agenda, revealing how environmental alarmism and "scientific consensus" have been deployed by globalists as a political instrument.

https://www.amazon.com.au/Green-Tyranny-Exposing-Totalitarian-Industrial/dp/1594039356

STRIVING FOR WORLD DOMINATION

A former British intelligence officer explains how the British elite have always worked towards world domination. The essence of their strategy is to create a worldwide crisis and then bring the answer.

They use orchestrated disasters like pandemics and climate change to further their goal of world domination. Psychological techniques are applied to get people to blindly obey their every command under the guise of "keeping everybody safe".

They are absolutely dependent on the world population remaining ignorant of their plans. They cannot rule those who refuse to be ruled.

https://stopworldcontrol.com/british/

WHAT IS THEIR FULL AGENDA?

The global elite's full agenda is so insane it sounds like a work of fiction, a mere conspiracy theory, but it's not! I wish it were! Instead, the evidence is all around us and easy to see.

The elite-controlled United Nations is a *wolf in sheep's clothing*. It is not a friend of humanity but the greatest deceiver in the history of the world.

Their puppet-politicians and media propagandists continually tell us that the most important things for humanity right now are environmental protection, digital IDs, Smart Cities and central banking. They are not!

The most important things are the end of war, provision of homes, food, clean water, work for all people, structured education for children, genuine care for the sick, and protection for the aged and vulnerable. That kind and loving humanitarian view is totally opposed to the elite's destructive environmentalism, dystopian depopulation plans and forced evolution into a cold and brutal transhuman, technological New World Order.

The full-blown dystopian nightmare being promoted by the United Nation's New World Order, *Revelation's clearly described Great Whore,* doesn't need to progress any further. It's time for this seventy-year-long nightmare to end. We can end it! All we need to do is rise up and take a firm stand against these dark forces and their fearful coercion, abuse, piracy and destruction of lives. Use the link below to see more evidence of their plans.

https://stopworldcontrol.com/domination/

SHOUT IT FROM THE ROOFTOPS!

The United Nations and its affiliates cannot continue to hide behind a facade of 'care and protection' pretending to promote world peace and unity while they tear the world apart.

- The United Nations was set up on the premise that it would ensure world peace. Has it succeeded? Not even close! Can it ensure future peace? No!

- Since it's inception, two of it's five permanent members, America and Russia have engaged in a decades-long cold war - a nuclear arms race that took the world to the brink of annihilation. If the goal of the UN were to promote peace, it would have outlawed weapons of mass destruction, but instead, more and more countries have, in response, armed themselves with nukes. Is the UN promoting peace? No! Under it's leadership, fear of nuclear war has become universal.

- Ukrane and Russia are both members of the UN. So, again, we see two UN members creating war and terror. Where is the peace? Where is the unity? Meanwhile, another permanent member, China, has threatened Taiwan. Why are the members of the UN instigating wars and fears of wars? World peace? I don't think so!

There is nothing 'united' or 'peaceful' about the United Nations. Instead, it has proved to be divided, divisive, manipulative, aggressive and dangerous!

Jesus said, *"A kingdom divided against itself will fall."* (Matt.12:22)

WHAT CAN WE DO?

Get behind the Senators and other politicians who are denouncing the UN | UNESCO | WHO | WEF alliance and calling for their defunding and the abandonment of their dictatorial agendas. Write to them. Actively show your support.

Flood social media with the truth. David Sorensen has made it easy with his well-researched blogs and invites everyone to share his blogs with family, friends and associates across the globe.

Separate yourself from the false teachers/ministers/leaders promoting the deceptive 'antichrist' propaganda within the churches. Tell them the truth.

Revisit the list of activities on page 170. Christians have the numbers and power to stop this tsunami of evil from doing any more damage, and a commission from our God to bring healing to a hurting world!

The 'New World Order' is the 'Old World Order' repackaged. *There is nothing new under the sun. (Ecc.1:9)* Will it succeed? No! And the elites know it! Their real interest is in the obscene amounts of money they stand to make before it collapses. Do they care about the suffering their greed causes? No! *"Come out from her, my people!"*

> *You are a chosen generation, a royal priesthood, a holy nation belonging to God, that you may proclaim the praises of him who called you out of darkness and into his marvellous light. (1Peter 2:9)*

Perhaps
you have come into
the Kingdom
for such a time
as this?

- Esther 4:14 -

www.ingramcontent.com/pod-product-compliance
Lightning Source LLC
Chambersburg PA
CBHW072101020426
42334CB00017B/1586